HOW TO USE COMMISSIONS

COMPENSATING

·DRAWS·BONUSES·PERKS·CONTESTS·

YOUR

TERRITORIES AND Q[...]

SALES

TO MOTIVATE THE SALES TEAM

FORCE

AND INCREASE SALES

W.G. RYCKMAN

PROBUS PUBLISHING COMPANY
Chicago, Illinois

Library of Congress Cataloging-in-Publication Data Available

ISBN 1-55738-085-6

Printed in the United States of America

2   3   4   5   6   7   8   9   0

CONTENTS

PREFACE

This book is about the compensation of a salesforce. It is written for sales managers up the line, from branch level to corporate executives.

A well-designed compensation plan for salespeople has two main objectives:

1. To reward salespeople so that their earnings will bear a direct relationship to the value of their contributions to the company.
2. To enable the company to stimulate its salespeople and to focus their efforts in directions that will profit them while helping the company meet its sales objectives.

That's all there is to it. To assist you in the development or the restructuring of your company's compensation plan we will explore various methods of paying salespeople, showing the strengths and weaknesses of each. We will discuss territories, quotas, salespeople's expenses, contests and policy decisions management must make.

It is my hope that you will find helpful suggestions in the book. Good luck to you, and good selling.

W.G. Ryckman

INTRODUCTION

Before commencing with the book proper, I would like to outline briefly my view of the basic relationship between salespeople and their bosses—the several layers of management that to a large extent control their destinies. To my way of thinking, salespeople and management are interdependent; one cannot exist without the other. Each relies on the other to achieve goals—corporate goals on the one hand, and personal goals for the individual salespeople on the other. What is good for the salespeople should be good for the company and vice versa.

In reading some of the literature on the subject it becomes apparent that not everyone agrees with my attitude. Management and salespeople are often cast in the roles of adversaries with opposing objectives. I cannot accept this approach. Salespeople rely on their earnings to support their families and themselves; corporations could not exist without an efficient means of distributing their goods. Neither can survive without the other.

Naturally, corporations feel they have the right to direct and control the activities of their representatives, and salespeople feel they have a right to equitable treatment. I do not find any area in such a relationship that could result in a basic difference between the two parties.

For each to understand the other's needs is essential, as is mutual trust and respect. Companies succeed because their workers are successful; salespeople are successful when the company supports them, that is, makes it possible for them to achieve their goals provided they work toward them conscientiously and in accordance with company policies.

Much of what I have to say in the book is colored by this attitude. I am on the side of the salesperson; at the same time I am on the side of the company. I can find no conflict or inconsistency in this stance.

CHAPTER 1
Compensation Plans— A Manager's Perspective

CHAPTER 1

Compensation plans for salespeople are designed to accomplish several objectives. Among these are: to assist the company in meeting its sales projections, to bring the earnings of the salesforce to desired levels; and to reward individual salespersons in direct proportion to their efforts and performance.

The objectives enumerated are closely interrelated; one cannot be considered while the others are ignored. Mutual interdependency, we might call it. To accomplish these worthy goals a compensation plan should be sound, equitable, as simple as possible and flexible.

Let's start by discussing corporate sales objectives. No two companies will have identical sales goals. The entrenched sales leader strives to hold his substantial share of market; a smaller competitor attempts to wrest away a few points of their market share. The large national company desires greater penetration in its districts; the smaller regional company engages in an expansion program to enter new sales markets.

To refine sales objectives even further we can suppose that to one company, increasing gross sales is a prime consideration. It may plan for a growth rate of 20 percent in each of the next five years. Another organization that is more concerned with profitability might seek to refine the mix of its products, emphasizing those with the larger gross margins.

Corporations have other goals allied to, but not directly connected with, the primary aim of selling their goods or services. New accounts may be a necessity, especially when a company changes from a skim to a penetration policy in a territory.

In some industries it is essential to expend time and effort in missionary work, which may produce no immediate reward but from which sales could benefit substantially in the future. For example, a health care company might develop a new toothpaste and a toothbrush both especially designed to serve the needs of eight- to twelve-year-old children. It would distribute thousands of samples to dentists, expecting them to be passed on to the parents of young patients making their regular visits. Sales generated by these free samples might reach impressive levels in the future if the dentists become convinced of the value of the products.

Rapidly expanding companies are constantly opening new territories. Some unfortunate organizations discover that reimbursed expenses of salespeople are getting out of line and require more control. Still others, even less fortunate, discover an alarming increase in bad debts written off, and must rely on the salesforce to help in correcting the situation.

A well-designed, well-administered compensation plan can be an important tool that, properly used, will provide invaluable assistance to a corporation in achieving its objectives, whatever they are. The compensation plan has other uses as well.

It is a major factor in the maintenance and development of a salesforce. A company succeeds or fails based on the performance of its salespeople, and the motivation and morale of these representatives are to a considerable extent influenced by the compensation plan adopted by the company. A secure salesforce, comfortable in its role and satisfied with its earnings, will be productive; a force inequitably paid under a poorly designed and administered compensation plan will not function in a manner satisfactory to its employer, nor will it be content with its earnings.

Sales managers are constantly looking for men and women to add to their salesforces. Each company has its own standards to control hiring practices. Among the qualities most frequently considered are ability, background, education, experience and in some instances age.

The compensation plan can be either a strong influence attracting the right type of person to the company or, conversely, an equally strong deterrent to joining a salesforce. If the company's plan is not competitive with the industry in which the company operates, the sales manager starts out at a disadvantage. He or she will be unable to hire desirable applicants, and must make do with those the higher-paying competitors have rejected.

Of equal if not greater importance to the sales manager is the necessity to retain personnel of proven ability. Salespeople will stay on the job if they are paid fairly and treated like human beings. Who can blame an individual for leaving one company for another that will pay 20 percent more for similar work? Consider the cost of losing an experienced salesperson. A replacement must first be found, then trained. Weeks or months must pass before the replacement gains familiarity with the assigned territory and the idiosyncrasies of each purchasing agent with whom he or she will deal.

In the meantime the previous salesperson will be doing everything possible to lure company customers to his or her new employer, your competitor. Losing a good salesperson is an expensive proposition and the cost is even more difficult to bear when the loss is due to a failure either in the company compensation plan or its administration.

The company should expect that a well-designed compensation plan will encourage the salesforce to achieve at least adequate sales performance. It should stimulate the men and women to do better for themselves. If this is accomplished, the company will benefit equally.

Finally, the plan should be so structured that performance is rewarded equitably. Compensation plans should relate payment with performance—no free-loaders, no exploited nice guys. Even a few individuals paid more than they are worth can wreck an organization, and the loyal, good employees who are doing a creditable job will sooner or later move on to fresher fields and greener pastures.

And don't forget, there are many aspects of performance. Sales production is highly important, of course, but other contributions are valuable as well. Training new hires, helping out in a crisis, loyally supporting the company, willingness to listen to and back the boss are all important in any organization. Superior contributions in these areas should be recognized and rewarded.

It is easy to measure the sales production of a salesperson. You are dealing with a tangible, finite matter and the proper compensation for performance is not difficult to determine. Yet, when you attempt to reward salespeople for the intangible services they render the organization, you encounter substantial difficulties. Management's judgments must be mainly subjective, and the mettle of a sales manager is severely tested when he or she must decide on the value of workers' contributions in these areas. However, they must be rewarded if the sales manager expects the organization to perform smoothly and effectively.

A number of authorities on the subject have expressed the opinion that a sales manager should strive to pay salespeople and women as little as possible and still keep them willing to do their jobs. In other words, don't pay a dollar more than you have to. Some pundits strike a high tone in defending such a stand. They talk of seducing people to work for money, contending their motivation should stem from the satisfaction of achievement on the job.

I am reminded of a story told of Herman Hickman who, for a time many years ago, coached the Yale football team. He was asked his reaction to losses and replied that it was all right to lose enough games to keep the alumni surly but not enough to make them openly rebellious. Well, Herman always enjoyed a laugh, but I find nothing humorous in the attitude of the authorities who adapt his philosophy on losses to compensation paid to a salesforce. I think they are wrong—dead wrong.

We have looked at compensation plans through the eyes of an employer, the corporation. Now let us consider how the salesperson regards them.

Sales managers advance from the ranks of the salesforce, and memories of their early days should be vivid enough to remind them of their hopes and aspirations when *they* sold for a living. What does the manager's own salesforce expect now, as far as money is concerned?

First of all they expect fair payment for performance. What is fair? Fair from whose point of view? Who says anything in this imperfect world must be fair? It isn't a very useful word when describing compensation.

What the salespeople conceive of as "fair" is probably receiving payment that is in line with that offered by the competition and commensurate with the quality of the jobs they do. If they sell in high volume, they feel entitled to high earnings; if they spend time training new salespeople, doing missionary work and making service calls, they should be recompensed for those activities.

They look for simplicity in a plan; they want to understand it fully and not run into unusual provisions that, to their way of thinking, have been introduced for the sole purpose of denying them what is rightfully theirs.

They like a plan that supplies them with a steady income at least on a minimum level to help them supplement occasionally small commission earnings.

"Fair" is not the only sticky word—another is—"contribution." How is contribution measured and evaluated? How many points for sales volume, training, attitude and all the other traits good salespeople are expected to exhibit? Join considerations of contribution with those of fairness as related to compensation and you compound the problem.

A salesperson wants a plan to be flexible. Some territories are more difficult to cover than others; some are rich, others comparatively poor. Plans should have the resilience to compensate for such differences that are out of a salesperson's control.

Last, but certainly not least, is a salesperson's conviction that any plan should provide an opportunity for him to improve his status: still higher earnings, a clear road to promotion.

How do salespeople's objectives relate to company goals? There should be, and in fact there are, no real areas of conflict. In the best of all possible worlds what is good for a salesperson should be good for the company. It doesn't always work out that way in details, but differences will not be insurmountable provided both sides are activated by a sense of equity and good will.

The company should appreciate the need for flexibility. The age of a man, and his years of service with the company and past contributions, are important factors that should not be ignored. Too much flexibility can be a handicap, too. A plan unique to every man would result in chaos. Basically, a standard plan is desirable, but the various elements of it should be subject to adjustment for special circumstances.

Above all, the plan any company adopts should be in line with the competition as regards total compensation. Except for compelling reasons to the contrary, a company would not structure its plan so that compensation would be 25 percent above or below its leading competitors in the field. In addition, a plan should be compatible with a company's ability to pay.

A final word. Once a company has determined the average level of compensation to be earned by its salespeople, or in a large organization by each class of salespeople, the prime consideration should be the total amount paid, not the basis on which it is paid. No matter how well a plan is designed, it is doomed to failure unless total compensation paid is competitive in the industry and represents equitable remuneration for services rendered.

The chart labeled "Attitudes toward a Compensation Plan" reiterates the points that have been made about the desirable elements of a compensation plan. The viewpoints of the salesperson have been contrasted with those of the company and it should be a surprise to no one that the interests of both parties are in almost every case entirely compatible. What is good for the salesperson is good for the company. There can be no fundamental conflict between men and management in a well-run organization. That is a good thought to keep in mind as you develop a compensation plan for your salesforce.

There are a number of ways in which a salesforce can be compensated ranging from salary to fringe benefits and perks. Each method can be employed to aid a company in achieving a desired result. Each has strengths peculiar to it, but none is an unmixed blessing. Unfavorable as well as favorable elements are implicit in each method of payment. In the following chapters we will discuss and analyze the most prevalent means of compensating salesmen.

Attitudes toward a Compensation Plan

Salespeople Look for	*Company's Attitude*
1. Adequate income for adeequate performance	1. No conflict, no argument on this point
2. Superior income for superior performance	2. None here either
3. Incentives for special achievement	3. All but a few reactionary companies agree
4. A base of fixed-income for security purposes	4. Many companies agree, but some cannot afford a fixed expense like salary. In certain industries compensation historically has ranged from 100 percent salary to 100 percent commission. Company attitude will depend on circumstances peculiar to it.
5. At least primary fringe benefits	5. No argument here, but not all companies can afford full range
6. Opportunity for advancement, promotion	6. As much to the company's advantage as the salesperson's
7. A yardstick to measure performance	7. Equally important for the company to measure performance

Attitudes toward a Compensation Plan *(continued)*

Salespeople Look for	*Company's Attitude*
8. Equitable treatment for all salespeople; pay based on performance—no free-loaders, no favoritism or exploitation	8. Equally important to the employer
9. A sense of security through the knowledge he is respected and regarded as a human being who is important to the company	9. Just as important to the company, which must rely on the morale of its sales-force. The sense of security and well-being of a sales-force pay many bonuses to an employer
10. Flexibility in a plan, sensitivity to changing conditions	10. Equally important to a company
11. Simplicity—easy to understand	11. The company agrees—the simpler the plan, the easier and cheaper to administer it

Hints to Sales Managers

- Be sensitive to the needs and aspirations of your sales staff.
- Remember that just as you control their success, so also do they control yours.
- In your relationships with your salesforce there is no substitute for straight dealing and equity.
- Be aware that the best compensation plan is the one that most accurately measures and rewards the performance of a salesperson.
- Utilize your compensation plan as a tool to aid you in meeting as many company objectives as possible.
- Above all, never lose sight of the fact that performance and earnings should go hand in hand.
- Realize that the company and the salesforce are not adversaries, but partners with nearly identical goals.

CHAPTER 2
Salary

CHAPTER 2

A straight salary payroll is by far the easiest for employers to handle. Deductions for Social Security, income taxes, health insurance and other fringe benefits are fixed and the workload is reduced to punching a few computer keys and writing a check once or twice a month.

In many industries this method of compensation is generally used and there is always an overriding reason for choosing a salary plan. Let us look at a few businesses using this method and certain types of selling best compensated by salary.

Highly Seasonal Industries

Consider a company whose major source of business is the sale of graduation rings and allied jewelry. Sales are concentrated in a short period in the spring and salespeople spend the balance of the year developing new accounts.

Under a salary plan, a salesperson's income will be spread evenly over the year, whereas if he or she were on commission they would be subject to long famines between short-term feasts. The company is obligated for fixed expenses during periods of low sales but the payment of regular salary effectively assures retention of salespeople.

High-Tech Industries

Salespeople for companies in this field are usually individuals of high caliber—well educated, highly trained and self-motivated. Often they have degrees in electrical or mechanical engineering, chemistry or other sciences. These individuals must be categorized as sales engineers. They spend much time advising customers, installing products and training users.

Companies believe (with reason) that representatives of this type do not require incentive pay as motivation to perform their duties. Salary, provided it is commensurate with contribution, is the ideal method of payment. It gives the employer full control over the activities of its salesforce, and the individual develops a sense of belonging to and importance in the company.

Trade Salespeople

This category includes those engaged in the distribution of products such as food and apparel who do little or no creative selling. Markets are well defined and the salesperson does not appreciably influence either the size of orders or the number of customers in the territory. In fact, he or she is often referred to as an "order taker."

Company advertising and promotion develop sales more effectively than the salesperson. Other than taking orders, about all he or she can contribute is setting up displays and restocking shelves. Both the company and the representative feel that a salary is the best compensation for such a job.

Route Salespeople

Beer and soft-drink salespeople as well as bread and milk delivery drivers are normally paid by salary. There is little they can do to increase sales or add customers on their routes, so a compensation plan involving incentives would not be of value either to the salesman or the company.

Missionary and Educational Salesmen

This type of salesperson does little direct selling to the company's ultimate customers, but rather encourages retailers to buy the company's products from the wholesaler or other organization through which it sells. Thus, a drug manufacturer's missionary force would urge druggists to order that firm's products from its wholesaler.

This kind of selling (if it can be called that) is low-key, and tangible results of missionary efforts are difficult to measure. There appears to be no alternative to the payment of salary to individuals employed in work of this sort.

Group Selling

In some manufacturing businesses selling requires a group effort involving a field man who generates interest in a product (often machinery, a complicated fabricated part or a raw material processed to rigid specifications), factory technicians, development engineers, managers who set prices and terms, installers and trainers at the customer's plant. When business is done in this fashion, many companies pay straight salaries to all their employees involved in the selling process. No other way of paying equitable compensation is practical. Salary paid to the different classifications of employees should be commensurate with the value of the services performed.

Many selling jobs other than those enumerated are compensated by salary. For some this method of payment is the best; for others a different payment base might be superior. When opening a new business, management should make a complete analysis of the disadvantages as well as the advantages implicit in a salary plan. When considering a change to salaried salespeople, an ongoing business should make an even more exhaustive study. There are strengths in salary plans, but there are weaknesses as well—for the employer as well as individual salespeople.

Salaried salespeople appreciate the security of a regular income. Orders seldom flow evenly and it is comforting to know a regular income will be received when sales production has fallen off during a slack period.

The security represented by a salary is a strong factor in lowering turnover in a salesforce. Management approves this aspect of a salary plan. It is not as happy, however, with the realization that the salary tends to keep weak, unproductive men on the payroll long after they would have disappeared had they been paid by commissions on sales made. The sales manager knows how difficult it is to terminate a salaried employee; it is one of his least pleasant duties.

Salary compensation is especially effective when a balanced effort is required of a salesperson. Generation of sales might be the primary responsibility, but other important duties such as missionary calls, training new employees, service work and so forth usually are required of the salesperson. The sales manager can require attention to these peripheral duties of a salaried salesperson since that salesperson draws part of his or her salary for performing them. Control over a salesforce is not always easy to maintain, but the ability to control salary is a major tool in the hands of a sales manager.

From a salesperson's point of view, the security that accompanies a salary is important and so also is the sense of belonging that comes with it. A salaried person feels he works for the company; a commission man may feel he is in business for himself and more often than not opposes any attempt to direct or control his activities. This problem is much less serious if the salesman is on salary. The distinction between the attitudes of salary and commission men may be mainly psychological, but it is nonetheless real.

A salaried salesforce limping along under weak management can destroy an organization quickly and completely. Without a firm hand on the tiller, many salaried salespeople tend to disregard their responsibilities and declining sales inevitably result. Salary can compensate effectively only when supervision is of high caliber and stimulating to personnel.

From management's perspective one of the greatest values of a salaried organization is the advantage it gives a company when it hires new people. A steady dependable income while learning a business is a great attraction to a potential employee. In addition to the tangible benefit, the new man feels that the company really considers him a valuable asset, one worthy of generous treatment.

Salary can also be helpful when new territories are being opened. It would probably take some time before a salesman could exist on the commissions from sales, especially when several months elapse between order and delivery. The same is true when an entirely new generation of products is introduced and a number of experienced men are assigned to establish the line.

On the other hand, there are basic weaknesses inherent in paying salesmen a straight salary. Salary is a fixed cost. It does not fluctuate with sales volume. A company approves a salary schedule based on what it believes to be an accurate projection of sales for the year. Suppose an unexpected event occurs or the economic environment worsens and sales drop 30 percent below expectations. Salary costs remain a constant, however, and selling costs rise to an unacceptable level—not an enviable position for a company to be in.

On the other hand, sales might show an unusual and sustained increase. In that case the company will profit from the fixed nature of salary expense. Yet, how long will the salesforce accept present salary rates in the light of substantially increased sales production? If raises are awarded, the next slump makes the problem even worse.

The chart below illustrates the effect on adjusted gross income when sales deviate from expectations and selling costs are fixed rather than variable expenses.

Sales	$100*	$130*	$70*
Cost of goods sold	80	104	56
Gross margin	20	26	14
Selling expenses	10	10	10
Adjusted gross margin	10	16	4

* All figures expressed in millions.

In all three examples cost of goods sold is 80 percent of sales. Selling expenses, consisting principally of salaries, remain at $10 million.

The effect of the fixed nature of selling expenses is readily apparent. When the company meets its projected sales volume of $100 million, the adjusted gross margin is 10 percent of sales. With a 30 percent increase in sales this figure jumps to $16 million, 12.3 percent of sales. When sales drop 30 percent the adjusted gross margin falls to $4 million, 5.7 percent of sales.

Had selling expenses been variable—say 10 percent of sales—adjusted gross margin with the increased sales would have risen only $3 million and declined a like amount when sales volume fell. Thus the fixed nature of selling expenses added an extra $3 million to margins when sales increased and cost the company an additional $3 million when they fell.

Another complaint of employers about the straight salary method of compensation is that it does not supply sufficient incentive to the salespeople to increase production. A person might be quite content with his or her earnings as they are. Why should he or she work harder for the company when there will be no direct benefit from the increased effort? If the salesperson expended more energy, his or her salary might be increased in the future, but it's a big if and how much of a raise could be expected anyway?

A properly administered salary plan makes frequent adjustments necessary. If too infrequent or niggardly, the effect would be to demotivate the salesforce. Conversely, if changes are made too often the salary becomes almost the same as commission with one important difference. Commissions rise in good times and fall in a recession. No problem arises when salaries are increased, but what sales manager enjoys the prospect of having to cut salaries and at the same time keep his salesmen motivated?

A fixed commission scale is one thing, adjustable salaries quite another. Very often raises are perceived by the salesforce as arbitrary and dictated by expediency. Capable management is essential and, even so, problems will inevitably arise.

In the eyes of many salespeople, the old-timers get paid too much, as do the underachievers that management is too soft-hearted to fire. The young tigers know they are underpaid. The feeling builds that time on the job and cronies in management have more influence in setting salary levels than production does. All this leads to frustration and frustration inhibits selling.

One final note. Employing a salaried salesforce when launching a new business is not recommended if financial resources are limited. Salary payments march along inexorably, dollar by dollar, while sales may at first be disappointingly slow. Analyze your bank balance and estimate cash flow in an ultraconservative manner before obligating yourself to a salaried salesforce. *Verbum sap*, as the Romans used to say.

The chart labeled "Analysis of Straight Salary Compensation Plans" below, itemizes the assets and liabilities associated with salary compensation of salespeople. Salary plans are neither all good nor all bad. Company circumstances and method of doing business must be taken into account before a salary plan is adopted or rejected.

Analysis of Straight Salary Compensation Plans

From Salesperson's Viewpoint   *From Company's Viewpoint*

STRENGTHS

Simple, uncomplicated	Simple, easy to administer
Stability of income	Reduces turnover in salesforce
Job security enhanced	Increases authority of sales
Sense of belonging to orga-	manager in controlling
nization	salespeople
	Makes it easier for management
	to secure cooperation of sales-
	people
	An effective tool when:
	Hiring new staff
	Introducing new product line
	Business is highly seasonal
	Large percentage of sales
	staff's time is spent in mis-
	sionary or educational work

Analysis of Straight Salary Compensation Plans
(continued)

From Salesperson's Viewpoint   *From Company's Viewpoint*

STRENGTHS

An effective tool when:
  Selling requires group effort
  Business is highly technical in
    nature and salesforce is of
    extremely high caliber
  Selling is mainly order taking
  Sales management is of proven
    superior ability

WEAKNESSES

Lack of incentive to excel,
  increase production
Salary increases seen as too
  small, too late, not based on
  performance but on favoritism
Old-timers, underachievers
  tend to be overpaid
Protection leaders often underpaid

Fixed expense, difficult to cut
Tends to keep inept on payroll
When leadership (management)
  is weak there is little incentive
  to increase sales
Frequent adjustments in salary
  are necessary, yet too many
  changes are as bad as too few
Financially weak companies are
  often unable to bear the expense of salaried salespeople
Requires excellent supervision,
  which is not always available

Hints to Sales Managers

- Check your company's finances. Can you afford salaried salespeople?
- Is your company's business cyclical in nature, especially sensitive to economic swings? If so, what effect could fixed selling costs have on your profits?
- Do any of your major competitors use a salary compensation plan? If not, why should you consider one?
- List your company's sales objectives. What will you gain by paying salary to your staff? What will you lose?
- Make sure you explore the other methods of compensating your staff before you make any decision on a compensation plan.

CHAPTER 3
Straight Commission

CHAPTER 3

eat advantage over paying
int of view. It is a variable
sales are made, commission
This keeps selling expenses

ments march inexorably on
costs can get entirely out of
a downward trend.

many other virtues. It is
severe cash shortage since
proceeds are received on a
sale.

Generous commission rates can be a strong incentive, an
element of much less influence under a salary plan, and many
organizations are successful because the salesforce enjoys a
liberal commission schedule. Commission-based compensation is favored by many companies to which sales volume is
of paramount importance and in which there is little activity
in such areas as missionary work or service. In many cases
sales volume written is the primary measure of the value of a
sales representative.

Some industries historically have taken the commission
route. Among them are real estate, automobiles, securities and
insurance. The reason for adopting the commission plan is
readily apparent.

Consider real estate agents engaged in selling residential

properties. They have only two major duties: to sell houses and to secure listings for their employer. Making a sale earns a portion of the commission payable; securing an exclusive listing means a clip when anyone sells the property.

Salespeople for a car dealership work the same way. Their job is to sell cars—they are not asked to wash them when they are received or repair automobiles damaged in fender-benders.

The value of such individuals to their employers is easy to determine—what they sell is what counts. Paying commission on sales is the only equitable way to reward them.

The same method of payment is usually chosen when a large portion of the salesforce is composed of part-timers or individuals who work an irregular schedule. In such cases, effective field supervision is not possible and control over selling activities is either weak or entirely lacking.

There is another group of men and women who are generally paid on a commission basis. Consider those employed in large numbers who sell their wares from house to house: brushes, household appliances, silver, cosmetics, kitchen appliances. Payment of salary would not be economically sound due to rapid turnover and lack of production on the part of many who are hired. Avon representatives are paid commission on sales. We are told there are 400,000 of them. Could any corporation afford to pay a salary to all those people?

Yet thousands of men and women earn substantial incomes through their efforts in door-to-door selling. They elect the freedom to work at their own pace that a commission base allows to the control over their activity inherent in a salary plan. Successful men and women in this area of selling are a special breed of people who take justifiable pride in their accomplishments.

I believe that we may correctly assume that a majority of people will work harder for sales when income depends on commission than when they are compensated by salary. I probably should modify that statement by adding that I refer to that group of men and women who are sufficiently self-motivated to want to better their social and economic status in life. Some people just won't respond to any stimulus, internal or external in origin. A salary that keeps a roof over their heads and groceries on the table satisfies them. Commission compensation supplies no incentive to such individuals.

Fortunately, however, another segment of our working population, and a large one, welcomes the opportunity selling offers them. They want to get ahead and to prosper, and a commission plan is the surest way for them to attain their goals.

Salary levels are to a large extent controlled by the overall performance of a company and the policies it operates under. The commissioned salespeople, on the other hand, are masters of their own fate. They can set goals and rely on their initiative and ability to reach them. In doing so they are largely independent of the varying fortunes of the company.

This type of salesperson requires more than motivation to enjoy success to the fullest extent. The outside commissioned salesperson needs a strong sense of discipline, a trait not always found in salespeople. Even if the sales manager is the best in the business, the salesperson spends most of the day alone. The salesperson decides on hours and schedules, punches no time clock, and is for the most part immune to the scrutiny of the boss.

Some people never learn how to discipline themselves, yet, without that ability jobs don't get done. An excuse can always be found not to undertake an unpleasant task. Commissioned salespeople lacking the ability to set their own standards as to work hours and level of dedication to the job will suffer unless an alert sales manager can act as their conscience. Alert, certainly, but the manager must be sensitive and perceptive too.

Even the best salesperson has barren spells when his or her most earnest efforts produce few positive results. During periods of depressed earnings household expenses continue on their merry way and even the most positive individual's can begin to doubt their ability.

The sales manager must exert a strong supportive influence when he or she observes that a person is going through one of these periods. It is also a manager's responsibility, while recognizing the independent feelings of the staff, to convince them that they really are a valuable part of the company and their contributions are fully appreciated. Occasionally even the best of salespeople nod (like Homer), but that luxury is denied to the top-rated sales manager.

The weaknesses of a straight commission method of compensation lie in the same area as the strengths of a salary plan. In like fashion the weaknesses of a salary plan are often the strengths associated with compensation by commission. (A chart listing the strengths and weaknesses of compensation by straight commission appears at the end of this chapter.)

A major weakness in a commission plan is that it makes hiring difficult for a company, particularly when training requires a protracted period without pay. Likewise, assignment of experienced men to new or undeveloped territories can cause serious problems. No one wants to sacrifice a steady income earned in familiar surroundings, even for the greater potential of a new location, if earnings will be sharply reduced for a period of several months or even longer.

These weaknesses in a commission plan are important for companies starting in business or those entering a program of expansion into new areas.

Whereas salary makes it easier to control an employee's activities, payment of commission diminishes the sales manager's authority. It is difficult for him to require the staff to do missionary work or even to concentrate on certain products that are more profitable for the company.

In good times, commissioned reps are inclined to skim their territory and ignore the necessity of developing new accounts for the future. Often salespeople will oversell customers in order to make a higher commission. This practice can result in customer ill-will and returns.

In short, commissioned reps may be more inclined to consider their own interests than those of the company. In combatting this tendency, sales managers earn a good part of their keep. Each salesperson is a different individual. No general course of action a sales manager can take will be effective with all employees.

This fact points up the necessity for the manager to know all that is to be known about his or her staff: what turns them on, what turns them off, what is the best way to reach each one of them. A sales manager must lead and guide, and to accomplish these essential tasks he or she must be respected.

Respect is such an important word and relates to such a vital attribute of sales management that we'll spend a few paragraphs discussing the concept. The sales manager needs the respect of the commissioned rep more than any other type of salesperson and the respect of that class of individual is the most difficult to win. Why?

Salaried reps realize that their superiors should be obeyed if they hope to progress in the company. Commissioned sales-people are often loath to acknowledge anyone's authority over them. Furthermore, because commissioned reps, being strong, supremely self-confident individuals, do not take kindly to control or anyone who attempts to exert it.

Yet if a sales manager is to be successful, he or she must be able to guide and direct the staff. A sales manager who is not respected cannot hope to achieve his or her aims. How does one gain respect?

I once knew rather well the president of a corporation that employed thousands of salesmen. He was a powerful man, a great salesman himself and a tenacious bulldog. He grabbed hold and never let go. Once I heard him say when speaking of his salesforce, "I don't care whether they like me or not, but I demand their respect." How wrong he was— nobody can secure respect by demand; it must be earned. In attempting to demand it my friend was no more effective than King Canute ordering the tide to halt its rise.

How does a sales manager earn respect? Here are the five basic factors I believe are involved in the process. Every sales manager should possess these traits.

Dependability

A sales manager's word must be his or her bond. No waffling or back-tracking can be tolerated. Once a decision is made and announced that is it—no ifs, ands or buts. Promises are kept. It adds up to strength of character.

Support

A manager must support the salesforce, backing individuals 100 percent when they are right, yet being equally firm in correcting them when they are wrong.

Honesty, Equity, a Sense of Fair Play

This trait implies no favoritism and equal justice for everyone. It permits no half-truths, but requires complete and open disclosure—telling it like it is, as the saying goes. Such an attitude begets trust, and without trust there can be no respect.

A Genuine Interest in People

The manager must have concern for employees and, along with that, compassion when disciplinary action must be taken.

Mastery of the Job

No one can truly respect a bungler, even a well-intentioned one. Sales managers should be effective, in control of themselves as well as the organization. They must be strong, not reluctant to take action when it is called for and at all times decisive—not afraid to take a stand.

Compensation by Straight Commission

From Salespeople's Viewpoint   *From Company's Viewpoint*

STRENGTHS

Incentive to increase income

Knowledge that they are
masters of their paychecks—
that they will be paid in
direct proportion to their
sales production

Knowledge that they are not
dependent on company policy
regarding raises

Knowledge that their earnings
do not depend on profit-
ability of the company

Knowledge that they can set
their own goals and profit from
meeting them

Commission is a variable, not a
fixed, expense

Selling expenses, as a function of
sales are controllable—an
advantage when cash
is scarce

It is a strong incentive to salespeople to increase production

A good plan when securing
orders is prime duty of
salespeople

Excellent for part-timers

WEAKNESSES

Lack of stable income causes
hardship in slack times

Requires a high degree of discipline in financial matters—a
quality not always found in
salespeople

Lack of income as a new hire is
trained or when opening a new
territory

Lack of feeling of belonging to
organization

Loss of control over salesforce

Diminished authority of sales
manager

Leads to skimming in rich
territories

Leads to overselling

Leads to ignoring of duties other
than selling

Salespeople inclined to place
their own interests above
those of company

May lead to an adversary
attitude between salespeople
and   management

Hints to Sales Managers

- Pay by commission if you employ a large number of part-timers.
- Commission plans rely heavily on the incentive factor—make sure salespeople know what successful selling can mean to them.
- Discover the key to people's motivation and use it to help them achieve their full potential.
- *You* are the sales manager. Manage your people—don't let them manage you.
- Offer advice and guidance in financial management to your salespeople.
- Above all, strive to earn the respect of every person in your organization.

CHAPTER 4
Commission Rates

CHAPTER 4

Historically, commission has been paid on sales volume. On a fixed commission base, an established percentage of sales volume is paid to a sales rep. Other plans call for increases in rate as volume increases. In still others, a regressive schedule decreases the rate as volume increases.

Fixed rate commission is easy to figure and administer. If the rate is 4 percent, it stays at that percentage whether the sales rep sells $20,000 or $200,000. The rate may be applied to dollar volume, gross margin, even unit sales—whatever base the company adopts.

A progressive commission rate accomplishes a major objective of most corporations: it provides a constant incentive to a salesforce to do better for itself. Consider this example:

	Sales	Commission Rate
Up to	$50,000	3%
From	$50,000 to $100,000	4%
Above	$100,000	5%

If a rep's quota is $75,000, he would earn $2,500 if he hit it exactly—a composite rate of 3.33 percent. If he sold $115,000, he would be paid $4,250—a composite rate of 3.7

percent. Superior pay for superior performance. Such a program makes sense. The more the company sells, the better it should do, and the more the salesperson sells, the greater should be his reward.

We must add a word of caution here, however. Salespeople are sharp—never forget that. If the rules allow a way to beat the system, salespeople will find it. They are just like any citizen preparing income tax returns; they'll take advantage of any legitimate opportunity to reduce their taxes before they sign the return.

Take this example: over a period of two months a woman sells a total of $150,000. If she is working under the schedule shown above, she would earn $2,500 each month if her sales were equally divided over the period. If, however, she should so arrange her orders that in the first month she reported $35,000 and in the second $115,000, her total earnings would be $5,300 ($1,050 for sales of $35,000 and $4,250 for sales of $115,000). The shorter the reporting period the greater the opportunity to rig the system. I agree, $300 is not equivalent to the national debt, but as found money it will pay a few bills.

At first sight a regressive commission plan under which commission rates decline as sales increase doesn't make sense. I cannot conceive that a rational plan would lower a man's composite rate the more he sold. It is difficult to understand how a company can ethically reap the benefit of higher sales at the same time it increases its profits at the expense of the salesman.

The following table illustrates the workings of a regressive plan. You will note it is the opposite of a progressive plan.

	Sales	*Commission Rate*
Up to	$40,000	5%
From	$40,000 to $75,000	4%
Above	$75,000	3%

Thus, a person selling $40,000 would earn $2,000 paid $3,400 (4.67 percent of sales), and on volume of $100,000 he or she would receive $4,150 (4.15 percent of sales). Note in the last example that while the first $40,000 in sales earned the salesperson $2,000, the final $60,000 earns only $2,150.

Yet, there are many advocates of a regressive system. Their first claim is that the system puts a brake on overselling and makes a rep more willing to handle the other responsibilities of the job such as missionary work and service calls. There may be some validity to this approach, but what is management for? Can't it control its men? It might be wiser for a company to hire a good sales manager than deliberately to put a curb on sales.

The advocates also say a regressive system tends to cause sales to flatten out, reducing the aberrations normally experienced. It would certainly be foolish for a salesman to lump his sales into a single pay period, but why use a sledge hammer to drive a tack? Management is the proper answer, not confiscation.

A third point is made that a regressive system is effective in industries where first orders are difficult to secure, but repeat orders are received almost automatically. In such a specialized industry it would seem more equitable to pay a substantial commission for an appropriate period of time on orders received from a new customer and a lower rate on reorders beyond that date.

Curiously, nowhere have I seen comments by advocates of a regressive rate plan on the reception given it by the individuals most concerned—the salesmen. I should think a sales manager would have a difficult time explaining the rationale of it to his staff.

The final and strongest argument advanced by proponents of a regressive system is that it prevents salespeople from earning too much money—so much they are reluctant to accept promotion, so much that they will make more than the sales manager and even higher company officials. We are told that the career-minded salesperson's ultimate goal is advancement to loftier levels of responsibility. This is undoubtedly true for many, but the most percipient and successful of them realize that promotion into management often occasions an exchange of income for prestige and authority.

Who ever said that the best salesperson made the best manager? Only in exceptional cases is this a fact. The super-salespeople are often loners, many of them selfish, thinking more of themselves than of their employers. They are reluctant to allow anything to interfere with their eternal quest for sales. They are disdainful of new hires, not eager to waste time helping those who soon will be out in the field making sales that they feel belong to them.

Many of the superstars exhibit traits directly opposed to those valued in a sales manager. This breed of salespeople can be egotistical and hard-headed. They do not suffer fools gladly. Make such a person a sales manager and you lose a top producer and take the chance of destroying a whole sales organization.

Let's go a little further. Where is it written indelibly that a top salesperson shouldn't earn more than the boss? If the coach of the Chicago Bulls earns a quarter of what Michael Jordan makes, I would be surprised. I hope no one tries to tell Jordan his salary should be scaled down so he can look forward to being promoted to coach some day.

The more reps produce the more they should be paid because for every dollar they make, the company makes several. Let the salesforce sell everything it can sell as long as the factory can supply the goods. If it can't, the salesforce will find a new home. The higher the level of sales the more profit the company makes even with a progressive commission plan.

Once overhead is covered, the incremental sales are the most profitable the company can make. Fixed costs being covered, the gravy becomes richer. The chart on the following page will illustrate this point. Perhaps I have oversimplified the figures, but the basic principle of the incremental approach is sound.

The corporation budget projected sales of $700,000 for the year at a factory production cost of $500,000. It expects to incur selling expenses of $140,000. The margin thus becomes $60,000. Factory costs include materials and direct labor of $200,000 and fixed overhead of a like amount.

XYZ Corporation

	Projected Results	20 Percent Increase in Sales
Material and labor	$200,000	$40,000
Fixed overhead	200,000	—
Variable overhead	100,000	20,000
Cost of goods sold	$500,000	$60,000
Sales	700,000	140,000
Gross margin	200,000	80,000
Selling expenses (20 percent of sales)	140,000	28,000
Adjusted margin	$60,000	$52,000

This type of overhead remains the same no matter what level of production is achieved. It includes property taxes on the factory, the salaries of the plant manager, engineers, department heads and office workers. Once these costs are covered, they cease to be a charge against factory production costs.

Further overhead amounting to $100,000 is variable in nature. In other words, it is a function of the level of production in the factory. Cost of power to run machines longer and cost of additional supplies are examples of overhead costs that will rise when more goods are produced.

Let us assume that company products were well received by customers and the salesforce did an excellent job, with the result that sales increased by 20 percent over projections. Material and labor on the increase would cost $40,000 and variable overhead would cost an additional $20,000. The fact that there would be no further expense for fixed overhead would result in a gross margin for the additional sales of $80,000.

If selling expenses remained at a constant 20 percent of sales, margin on the incremental sales of $140,000 would be

$52,000 against a margin of $60,000 on the base sales of $700,000. Even if selling expenses increased by 25 percent on the incremental sales from $28,000 to $35,000 (a large increase even under a progressive commission rate), the additional margin of $45,000 would be 32 percent of the incremental sales. On projected sales of $700,000 the margin of $60,000 is 8.6 percent of sales.

If the regressive commission advocates held sway in XYZ Corporation, we could expect to see selling expenses on the incremental business reduced below $28,000 and the adjusted margin would increase by a like amount.

The economics of the situation lead me to favor doing whatever can be done to increase sales rather than making a strong effort to inhibit growth. And I don't understand why the salesforce should be denied the right to enjoy its share of the additional profits it helped the company to earn.

No sales manager ever forgets the value of a great example: "If so-and-so can do it, so can you." Salespeople profit from their own success; sales managers profit from the success of their staff; and companies profit from the success of every employee.

Salespersons and sales managers are not clones—don't ever forget that. They operate on two different sets of values. It is quite possible that the best sales manager was never an outstanding salesman. Attributes other than the ability to sell in high volume are required to make him a successful manager.

Years ago I had a top division manager, one of the finest men I ever knew. He was a great salesman, but he had the compassion and interest for his branch managers and salesmen that set him well apart from his peers. He had built a remarkably productive area of the country from absolutely nothing by his innate ability, personality and drive. His pay was based on the volume and profitability of his division.

One day the president of the company called me, saying he would be retiring soon and the board of directors had authorized him to offer the job to Obie, my division manager. The president, Paul, was polite enough to ask my permission before speaking to Obie. I told him to go ahead, but that Obie would turn him down, not revealing my reasons for the statement. Paul was highly indignant—who wouldn't give an eye tooth to be president? We bet a dinner at Brennans in New Orleans on the outcome.

Three days later Obie called me. "The damndest thing happened," he told me. "Paul called me to New York and offered me the presidency of the company. How do you like that?" "What did you tell him?" I asked. "I turned him down," Obie responded. "Why?" "Too many administrative duties, board meetings and all that. Two, I didn't think I was qualified to handle the job. I'm not a great intellect. All I know is people. Third, I didn't see why I should take a $100,000 cut in pay just to be president."

Enough said on the subject except that Obie joined Paul and me in New Orleans and Paul picked up the tab for a superlative dinner.

Commission Based on Gross Margin

As time goes on, companies are giving ever greater attention to the profit margins of the products they sell. They are breaking away from the long-held conviction that increasing gross dollar volume is the ultimate sales objective. An important result of this shift in thinking is the growing trend toward giving weight to the relative profitability of products when establishing commission rates. To bring this about they introduce the gross margin concept. Simply stated, gross margin is sales price less cost of goods sold. A few figures will illustrate my point.

Product	Gross Margin	Sales	Margin	5 Percent Commission	Net Margin
A	40%	$150,000	$60,000	$7,500	$52,500
B	20%	150,000	30,000	7,500	22,500

Product A carries twice the margin of Product B, yet a company paying commission on sales volume would reward salesmen equally no matter which product they sold. The margin, minus commission, of Product A is two and one-third times that of Product B.

If the company changed to the profitability concept as its basis of commission, it might pay 6 percent commission on sales of Product A and 4 percent on B. The Product A salesman would receive $9,000 commission and the other salesman would be paid $6,000. Reward would be more in line with the value of the sales to the corporation. The net margin on Product A, $51,000, would be more than twice the $24,000 net on Product B.

Companies paying commission on a gross margin basis should not lose sight of the importance of sales of high-volume products, even though they carry low margins. Overhead is spread over production costs and the sale of high-volume items contributes heavily to the absorption of fixed costs.

Two methods are employed to pay commission on the gross margin basis. The first is to list the margin of all products and provide each salesman with a copy. The overriding disadvantage of this method is that the salesmen are privy to information the company undoubtedly regards as confidential. Yet, salesmen would consider withholding this information from them unacceptable. Without it, how could they check the accuracy of their paychecks?

The second method avoids this dilemma. The full line of products is divided into groups, depending on their gross margins. Commission rates would be highest for the most profitable category. Here is an example of what might be done.

The salesperson is told the classification of each product and the applicable commission rate, enabling her to confirm the accuracy of her commission statement. Her commission is, of course, based on gross sales volume rather than gross margin, but the effect of this method of payment is to reward the salesperson for selling the more profitable items. She is not aware of the gross margin of individual products. All she

Product Group	Gross Margin	Commission Margin
A	Over 50%	4.5%
B	40–49%	4.0%
C	30–39%	3.5%
D	Below 30%	3.0%

knows is that a certain item is class A and when she sells it her commission rate is 4.5 percent.

It would be incumbent on the company to review constantly the costs of all products and keep groupings up to date. Switches from one category to another would have to be announced immediately to the salesforce.

There are many advantages to this method of paying commission regardless of the breadth of the lines offered by a company. No matter what method of payment is employed, it is essential that the salespeople have a clear and complete understanding of it.

Straight Commission Plans

From Salesperson's Viewpoint   *From Company's Viewpoint*

FIXED COMMISSION RATE

Incentive to increase production   Encourages salesforce to higher
Easy to understand   sales level
Few disputes   Easy to administer
                                       Simple to explain

Straight Commission Plans *(continued)*

From Salesperson's Viewpoint   *From Company's Viewpoint*

PROGRESSIVE RATE

Even stronger incentive to sell
Opportunity to schedule orders
  in pay periods advantageous
  to salesperson

An effective tool in increasing
  sales
Results in additional selling
  costs, which should be absorb-
  ed by higher sales volume
Requires strong management
  to prevent abuses in:
    1. Manipulating orders
    2. Overselling

REGRESSIVE RATE

Advocates claim it should encourage salespeople to get promoted out of selling and into
  management
Note: In all fairness, some
  companies operate in an environment in which a regressive rate system is superior to
  other methods of compensation. It will be the obligation of
  the sales manager to determine
  whether his company is a
  member of that group.

Advocates claim it:
Reduces threat of overselling
Makes reps more amenable to
  handle job responsibilities
  other than selling
Evens out peaks and valleys in
  sales
More accurately rewards selling
  efforts when first sales are difficult to secure, but reorders
  are to great extent automatic
Prevents salespeople from
  earning too much money

GROSS MARGIN BASE

Encourages sales reps to make
  more money by selling high-
  margin products
Will please those who do sell
  this type of product; will dis-
  please those who don't

Incentive to sell more profitable products benefits company
Amount of commission paid by
  company is more closely related to value of sales to the
  company
Reward more nearly approxi-
  mates contribution

Straight Commission Plans *(continued)*

From Salesperson's Viewpoint   *From Company's Viewpoint*

GROSS MARGIN BASE

Could result in closer relationship with company; reps are
  made aware of what sales are
  of greater benefit to the company; what benefits the company benefits them also.

Hints to Sales Managers

- Check all commission plans before choosing one.
- Your prime responsibility is to your company, but don't forget your staff relies on you to represent their interests firmly and fairly.
- Sometimes it does pay to spend a buck to make one, two or three.
- Remember your interests are basically the same as your staff's. All of you are trying to succeed and it takes a mutual effort for everyone to achieve their goals.
- The more you do to relate contribution to reward, the better is the job you do for your company and your staff.

CHAPTER 5
Manufacturer's Representatives, Independent Contractors and Distributors

CHAPTER 5

Many companies find it economically infeasible to maintain a conventional salesforce in all of their selling areas. Perhaps a section of territory is so large and sparsely populated that the expense of covering the widely scattered potential accounts would be exorbitant considering the sales that might be obtained. Yet, business is available in the area and would be profitable if an inexpensive method of coverage could be employed.

Other companies of limited resources might sell a narrow range of inexpensive products. To them an average order is small and a salesman would have to write an impossibly large number of tickets to make a living. His traveling expenses would be high and his earnings seriously limited. The business he might obtain would be profitable neither to him nor his employer. Once again, the sales are there; the problem is to secure them and at the same time make a profit.

In still another case, a company's sales might be highly seasonal by nature, with nearly all of its volume coming during a relatively short period of three or four months. Consider, for example, the monthly sales graph of a swimming pool supply company operating in northern New England. A ski equipment manufacturer selling in the same area would have a sales drought lasting from April through October.

If we consider also another company that specializes in seeds and home garden tools and a fourth that concentrates on pennants and souvenirs to be sold at college football games, we would cover a year during which there would be a steady demand for at least one group of the products we have described.

A conglomerate owning all four companies could operate successfully with its own salesforce provided the men were resilient enough to shift selling gears every three or four months.

A salesperson representing a single company would starve unless he or she could hibernate for a least two-thirds of the year. Even then, unlike a bear, he or she would have to pay the mortgage and insurance premiums each month, heat or cool his or her den and render to Caesar's tax collector his due.

Yet, companies do have the means to earn welcome profits despite the conditions described above. They use manufacturer's representatives, independent contractors or distributors. The first two have much in common, the major difference being that in most cases an independent contractor sells the products of one company while the manufacturer's representative, as the name implies, sells for several companies.

Quite often independent contractors are fully or semi-retired former employees of a company who work a few hours a week to supplement retirement income. Manufacturer's reps, usually full-time salespeople, customarily handle noncompeting products of the companies they represent, supplying a varied line of items in demand by their customers. Some reps deal in raw materials or supplies used by industrial factories, others sell to retail establishments such as hardware stores. Still others might carry supply items for motel or fast-food chains. It would be unusual to find a manufacturer's rep who dealt with more than one type of consumer. In general, they sell only to customers of similar classification and requirements.

Manufacturer's reps and independent contractors are usually individuals who operate without the benefit of support personnel. Only in exceptional cases do they maintain an inventory of the merchandise they offer. When orders are secured they are forwarded to the corporation for filling. Bill-ing can be made by either party. Reps are compensated for no expenses and are paid on a straight commission basis. They usually operate in clearly defined territories and are granted exclusive rights to all sales emanating from the area.

Distributors operate quite differently. Often they maintain fully equipped general offices, employ a number of salesmen and operate sizable warehouses containing an inventory of commodity type products of the companies they represent. Like the manufacturer's reps, they receive no expense allowance and are paid either by commission or a system of discounts on the products they handle.

When Social Security coverage was enacted in the 1930s, many companies exempted outside salesmen on the basis that they were independent contractors. They claimed that turnover in this group of salespeople was high, part-timers were the rule rather than the exception, recordkeeping was highly onerous and expensive. Later, general opinion toward Social Security changed and the vast majority of outside salespeople were brought into the system. To this day, however, a few independent contractors remain—an isolated and seemingly endangered species.

Independent contractors are exactly what the name implies. They are independent, sometimes excessively so. As they represent a single company, it is possible to exert a modicum of control over them, but by the nature of their business they are masters of their fate. One advantage they have over manufacturer's reps from the company point of view is that their efforts are not divided among the products of a number of companies. The one company they represent is assured that whatever effort they expend is expended for its benefit.

A few more words on manufacturer's reps and distributors, the major source of sales not obtained through company employees. The sales manager who controls, or more precisely, who attempts to control their activities is confronted by a number of problems, some administrative and others motivational.

Early on, the manager realizes that independent agents do not have the loyalty one would expect from employee salespeople. Such agents often serve many masters. Length of relationship might exert a positive influence, but fundamentally agents' hearts are in their pocketbooks and the lines most profitable to them command their greatest attention. Even if the manager's line is the most valuable to an agent, the manager is still not home free; if the line is in a less important category, his or her problems are multiplied.

The sales manager's primary objective is to make it as easy as possible for the agent to make money by selling in volume. To do this he or she must provide training in the use and application of the products and assist in developing selling techniques. No agent can sell successfully items he or she does not understand fully.

Agents are busy people. Many masters impose a multitude of demands on them and it is not always easy for the sales manager to schedule enough time with new reps to make them familiar with the manager's line and, once that is done, to keep them abreast of developments and changes in the line. Constant communication with the agent is essential, as are visits to the field.

The most frequent complaint voiced by sales managers is that agents do not spend enough time promoting their particular company's products. A legitimate complaint, it is true, but consider the plight of the agent. He or she represents a dozen clients and each demands 20 percent of his time. This conflict illustrates the fundamental problem inherent in selling through independent agents.

Sales managers also feel that agents do not spend enough time developing new accounts. Again a justifiable concern, but in this respect are agents much different from company-employed salespeople?

Put it this way: basically sales managers throws their products into a pot with many other noncompeting items. They hope the agents will give them a square deal and attempt to encourage this by paying a generous commission, training the agents to the extent they will accept direction and keeping in as close touch with them as possible. The results obtained will depend on how successful the manager's efforts are and the quality of the person chosen to represent the company.

Despite the difficulties in operating with manufacturer's reps and distributors, this method of selling has advantages when it is uneconomic for a company to use its own salespeople in an area. The costs of selling by independent agents are entirely variable. No costs are incurred until a sale is made. The amount of commission is fixed and the company is not obligated to defray any selling expenses of the agent.

Thus, all sales made should be profitable. To secure them the sales manager assumes additional responsibilities and extra duties, but he or she is paid to do the job and it includes managing independent agents.

Use of Manufacturer's Agents, Independent Contractors and Distributors

BENEFITS

Enables company to cover territories that will not support a salesperson because:
1. Potential too low
2. Company products low in price and average sale small
3. Business too seasonal to support a salesperson

All sales made should be profitable because:
1. Company's only obligation is to pay commission on sales
2. No other selling expenses are reimbursed

PROBLEMS ENCOUNTERED

Lack of control over activity of agents
They may have little loyalty to your company
A negative influence will be encountered if your products are merely an unimportant sideline to the agent
It is difficult to:
1. Develop an aggressive sales attitude on the part of agents for your products
2. Instruct agents on products and selling techniques
3. Spend time in the field with them
4. Encourage them to canvas for new accounts

Use of Manufacturer's Agents, Independent Contractors and Distributors   *(continued)*

    5. Secure adequate selling time for your products
    6. Select the most effective agent

Frequent communication with agent may be difficult to maintain
Heavy demands are placed on the time of the sales manager

Hints to Sales Managers

- Be selective in choice of agents.
- Investigate character and references thoroughly.
- Check other products handled.
- Check caliber and reputation of other companies represented.
- Will your line be a major component or relatively unimportant to the agent?
- Does the general line of products carried by the agent indicate that he or she now sells to customers who are potential users of your products?
- Are there many potential users of your products in the area with which the agent has had little or no contact? If so can he or she be relied on to generate business for you from them?
- Once an arrangement for representation has been made:

  do everything in your power to instruct the agent in the specifications and uses of your products;

  provide as much sales training as possible so your products will be presented to customers in the best light;

  maintain constant communication with the agent;

  spend time in the field with the agent, especially with the object of opening new accounts; and

  keep the agent abreast of new developments in your company—new products, sales techniques and so forth.

CHAPTER 6
Drawing Accounts, Bonuses, Profit-Sharing, Fringe Benefits

CHAPTER 6

W e've already talked about salary and commissions and digressed for a few minutes discussing reps and distributors. Now we'll return to further consideration of other forms of compensation for salespeople.

Drawing Accounts

The use of drawing accounts negates to a considerable extent the lack of security felt by persons paid on a straight-commission basis. A nonguaranteed draw is really nothing but an advance against earnings. Shortages not covered in lean months are recoverable from income in richer ones. Accounting is continual and overdrafts are never forgiven.

A guaranteed draw is similar to a minimum salary, and failure to cover the draw is forgiven at the end of the accounting period, usually one year. Thus, a man who failed by $2,500 to cover his draw in the course of a calendar year would have the shortage written off and start the new year even with the board. Had he been on a nonguaranteed draw, the overdraft would continue to hang over his head until repaid.

Drawing accounts are effective in highly seasonal businesses in which salespeople's earnings are concentrated in a few months and long arid spells are normal. They are also excellent for starting a new hire in business. Some companies put recruits on a guaranteed draw for a period of time, switch them to a nonguaranteed draw when they should be able to earn their keep and finally put them on the regular company compensation plan when their apprenticeship has been completed.

Salespeople would, of course, much prefer a straight salary to a drawing account as they learn a business. For that matter they would prefer a salary over a drawing account at any time. There are no strings attached to a salary. A salesperson paid a combination of salary and commission keeps every dime he or she gets paid. Exchange the salary for a draw and it's a whole new ball game.

Other types of earnings such as commission, bonus or profit sharing are usually included in a compensation plan featuring a draw and the draw is charged against them before final settlement is made with a salesperson. There is a feeling of permanence about a salary that is missing in a draw. Yet, it is easier to switch people from either type of draw to commission than it is to take away their salary and require them to support themselves from then on through their commission earnings alone.

As a matter of fact, companies that do shift from salary to commission plans experience a larger than normal turnover of salespeople. As might be expected, many who leave the company are the lower producers who would suffer a severe drop in earnings as a result of the change. Drawing accounts against commissions focuses attention on the importance of selling to earn a livelihood.

Bonuses

The eye of every sales rep lights up at the magic word *bonus*. Paying a bonus is a method a company adopts to reward special contribution and as an incentive to superior performance. Surveys have indicated that more than half the companies paying bonuses pay them annually, one-fourth pay quarterly and the balance is almost equally divided between semi-annual and periods under three months.

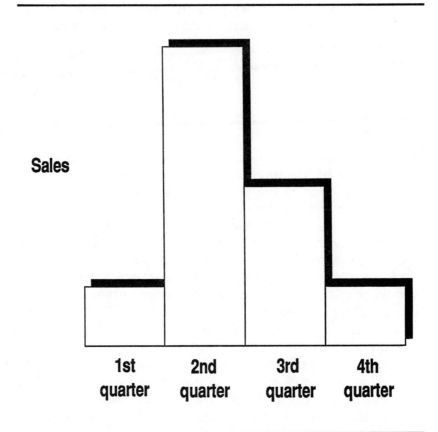

Sales

| 1st | 2nd | 3rd | 4th |
| quarter | quarter | quarter | quarter |

The annual period has much to recommend it. To earn bonuses, salespeople must apply themselves to the job for a whole year and there is less reason to manipulate sales than there would be were the bonus based on production over a shorter period. In seasonal industries or those with frequent peaks and valleys the longer period would appear to be preferable. A simple chart will illustrate this point.

With a sales pattern similar to the one shown, a company that offered a standard quarterly bonus would pay through the nose in the second quarter and probably no salesperson would reach bonus-earning production in any other period.

The company should either base the bonus on sales for the entire year or establish different quotas for each quarter. The purpose of a bonus is to reward a salesperson for doing a good job for the company. Bonuses that are too easily earned do not benefit the company and those that are impossible to attain do no one any good.

Discretionary Bonus

A discretionary bonus is one declared out of company profits. The amount of the appropriation depends on the success of the company during the preceding year and is subject to the approval of company executives or the board of directors. There is an element of uncertainty about this type of bonus; the company may have just completed a profitable year, but the directors may be concerned about the coming one and decide a conservative policy, particularly with regard to cash, should be adopted. Thus the normal bonus appropriation may be cut. On the other hand, a company might, despite less-than-satisfactory recent results, appropriate a substantial sum for bonuses if the future looks better.

The element of uncertainty is the principal weakness of a discretionary bonus. Since determination of interim profits is uncertain, most organizations that pay bonuses of this type use the entire fiscal year as a base, paying bonuses a month or two after the close of the year.

Once an amount has been set up in a bonus pool, it is necessary to distribute it as equitably as possible. Again the element of uncertainty is present. An example will illustrate this point.

Suppose a company appropriates the sum of $1 million to be distributed to its salesforce as a bonus. The country is divided into seven regions that contain a total of twenty-six divisions, each of which has several branches. The number of salesmen totals approximately 1,200.

How is that sum to be distributed? Good question. Does each region get one seventh of the bonus pool? That might be equitable provided all regions were of comparable size and performed equally well, but it's a sure bet they weren't and didn't. Should the money be allocated by division or even branch in accord with ranking depending on percentage of quota reached? A good approach, but what about the top salesperson in the whole company? She was the only good producer in her branch, but despite her record performance the branch ranked well below average.

Should branch managers submit lists of worthy candidates for a bonus to division managers who would consolidate and forward them to regional managers who would send them along to the vice president of sales at the home office who would make the final decision? If the vice president were a diligent and conscientious and studied all the recommendations submitted, the lucky recipient of a bonus would be fortunate to receive a bonanza in time to celebrate at a family reunion picnic on the Fourth of July.

All this indicates that it is not easy to distribute a discretionary bonus in a fair and timely fashion when a large number of salespeople are involved. A company with only ten or twenty salesmen finds the solution simpler. A much more accurate distribution can be made, but other problems replace the ones that have been avoided.

Do old school ties influence the distribution? How important is age, sex, years of service or cronyism in determining the amount of an award? When a subjective judgment is made, a charge of favoritism is never far behind. The unfortunate result is that even though the allocation was made with the judgment of a Solomon it will not be so perceived by a large segment of the salesforce. When bad feelings are created, the effect on an organization is immediately apparent. Morale drops and so do sales.

A sales manager who decides to divide the bonus allocation of his or her branch equally among the staff will fare no better. The higher producers will scream that they have been robbed while the new and weaker salespeople will applaud the manager's wisdom.

Unless discretionary bonuses are distributed under an accurate, fair and clearly understood plan they can do as much harm as good. The secret is to develop criteria on which to base the award. We'll go into this more deeply when we summarize our conclusions on bonuses.

Fixed Bonus

The fixed bonus is regarded as an extra reward for special performance and can be built into each salesperson's compensation agreement. Quotas are often used to determine fixed bonus awards.

A graded scale of bonus credits might be given for meeting or exceeding quotas. Bonus might start at 90 percent of quota, paying a modest amount for reaching that figure. For each 5 percent sold above that level the bonus would be figured at rates that would increase as each new plateau was achieved. An example of how such a plan might work is shown below.

(I should make it clear that the figures in this and other tables appearing throughout this book are not offered as recommendations for your use in setting up a compensation plan. The purpose of the tables is to outline a method of developing a plan to meet the needs of your company. The figures are for illustrative purposes only.)

Salesman A—Quota $250,000

Bonus for reaching   90 percent of quota = ¼ percent of sales
Bonus for reaching   95 percent of quota = ½ percent of sales
Bonus for reaching   100 percent of quota = ¾ percent of sales
Bonus for reaching   100 percent of quota = 1 percent of sales
(Continue as far as you like)

The bonus might also be figured based on gross earnings. Each year when the sales manager reviewed with a sales rep his or her quota, projected earnings for the period would have been calculated. The salesperson would earn a bonus for reaching 90 percent of that figure and each increment above that would be rewarded, the amount increasing as each level of earnings was reached.

Let us assume salesperson A in the example was expected to make $25,000 if he or she met the quota of $250,000. The bonus plan could be set up this way:

Salesman A—Projected earnings $25,000

Bonus when earnings reach	$22,500	$ 500
Bonus when earnings reach	$23,750	700
Bonus when earnings reach	$25,000	1,100
Bonus when earnings reach	$26,250	1,500

(Continue as far as you like)

The plans differ in one respect only: one bonus depends on achievement relative to sales quota and it would appear that the approach taken would matter little, but further analysis discloses a fallacy in this thinking. Consider one salesperson paid on a straight amount half of whose compensation is provided through salary. We would identify the major responsibility of the former as generating sales—either bonus plan would be equally suitable. What about the latter, many of whose activities are focused in other areas than selling and who therefore has a comparatively low sales quota? To base a bonus solely on sales in this case would be a mistake. This person might earn a large bonus by neglecting other duties and concentrating on sales. On the other hand, sales production might be little better than adequate but he could make extremely valuable contributions in discharging his non-selling obligations. He would receive no bonus unless a method of assessing his total effort were designed.

If criteria other than sales are important in determining the value of an employee's contribution, the bonus might be divided into two portions. The first would depend on sales

production and the second on performing other responsibilities: missionary calls, opening new accounts, training
new men, service work and so forth.

The bonus allocated to sales would be based on quota
and the formula used to compute it should be thoroughly understood by the rep. The other part of the bonus would perforce depend partly on quantifiable activities, such as opening
accounts and training new hires, and partly on the best subjective judgment of the sales manager when there is no way to
measure performance mathematically.

It should be the aim of management to remove, as much
as possible, subjective judgments in determining the amount
of a bonus. The more uncertainty that can be taken out of a
bonus policy, the better for everyone involved.

We are told that two-thirds of companies base bonuses on
attainment of quotas, either dollar volume or gross margin.
The remainder use new accounts, reduction in selling expenses, management conception of value of contribution made,
group performance or other criteria to control distribution. In
some cases a combination of criteria determine the amount of
bonus to be paid.

Office Bonus

It is not unusual for a branch or a district to win a company
bonus for meeting or exceeding its quota. Ordinarily such
sums are relatively modest in amount and sales managers
may distribute bonuses at their discretion. They might throw
a banquet for the whole organization, use the money as a
prize fund or distribute a portion of it to those who had done
a special service in the past year for which they received no
direct compensation. They might even decide to reward members of the office staff who had been instrumental in the success of the organization.

General Discussion on Bonuses

A word of caution. Fixed bonuses are paid irrespective of the
performance of the company. Company sales and profits may

be down, but a handful of talented salespeople will probably sail by their quotas and earn substantial bonuses. These payments will increase selling expenses to an extent determined by the number of people who do exceed quota. Perhaps this might be considered unfortunate from the company point of view, but the cost is minimal compared with the even worse results if no one sold enough to earn a bonus.

Of a more serious nature are the problems encountered when a company deliberately keeps salaries and commissions low and customarily pays a substantial discretionary bonus to bring earnings to projected levels. All salaries are a fixed expense and companies attempt to keep them to a minimum on the theory that it should seldom if ever be necessary to cut them in bad times. From the point of view of the company this approach has many advantages, but how does the salesperson react when the year-end bonus is cut in half because the company has suffered a disappointing year?

Salespeople unconsciously consider the customary bonus to be an integral part of disposable income, as fixed as their salary. They go into debt during the year and let bills pile up knowing that all will be well on February 1 when bonuses are received. The reduced payment leads to financial disaster and emotional trauma.

The executive or the committee that distributes discretionary bonuses is always subject to charges of prejudice and favoritism. At times the charges may be well founded. It is difficult if not impossible to devise a method of payment that rewards each person in an administrative position equitably and accurately. Personal judgment must be relied on, but when nearly absolute measures of performance are available, as in the case of salespeople, it makes sense to use them.

Profit-Sharing

Many experts in the field of sales management disapprove extending profit-sharing to salespeople. For once I agree with them. There may be an argument in favor of such a payment if no bonus plan is established for excellence in sales performance. When an adequate plan is or can be put into effect, however, profit-sharing is redundant.

Who can determine the precise source of additional or unusual company profit? Sales were up, probably, but why were they up? Extra hard work on the part of the salesforce? Possibly, but equally possibly the rise might be attributed to substantial cost savings in manufacturing that enabled the company to hold or even reduce price levels. Research may have developed a product superior to anything offered by the competition. The board of directors might even have lopped a few million off the payroll by getting rid of dead wood at the home office.

If management wishes to reward the men and women who brought about the higher profit, let it discover what and who was responsible and reward the deserving individual or group. Sales reps will benefit from improved products they sell at more competitive prices.

At times corporate accounting is so sophisticated that regional, division and even branch profits can be determined accurately. When dependable profit information is available it would be unusual if a regional manager did not have a profit-sharing clause in his or her contract and the same could be said for division managers. Often the pie is cut carefully enough that a slice is made available to branch managers who stand high on the profit list.

This practice I applaud. If an outstanding job is done, the individuals responsible should be rewarded. Profit-sharing paid to a branch manager is different from a bonus given a branch office. If a branch is profitable the credit should go to its manager, and to reward the success of his or her efforts is fitting and proper.

What happens when one or two branches or even divisions are highly profitable even though overall the company suffers near disaster in a year? The ability of the company to pay cannot be ignored and if profit-sharing were payable on a discretionary basis the individuals involved might receive little or nothing for their efforts.

On the other hand, had a policy been adopted under which all managers—regional, division or branch—received a fixed percentage of the profit made in their offices they would be paid irrespective of the condition of the company.

Profit-sharing, like bonuses, can be either discretionary or fixed. Choosing one method or the other can cause complications for each of the parties involved.

Fringe Benefits

Fringe benefits have become a fascinating subject and an item of considerable expense to a corporation. The costs of fringes vary to as high as 40 percent of direct compensation expense, depending on what benefits are offered and whether a portion of the expense is shared with the employee.

There are people alive today, and I confess I am delighted to be numbered among them, who remember when their job paid $25 a week and the weekly envelope actually contained two tens and a five-dollar bill. Think of it: Social Security deduction, no federal or state tax deductions. Hospital insurance was unknown, as were a majority of the fringes that are commonplace today.

Historically, salespeople were the last group to participate in the fringes made available by companies to their employees. Many benefits were introduced during the early Roosevelt years, around the time Social Security legislation was enacted, when outside salespeople were not considered in the same way as office or factory employees.

Salespeople were reluctant to change their long-established reputation as mavericks. Surveys made in the Fifties and Sixties disclosed that they preferred more generous commission rates to the fringes offered to others by their companies. However, times have changed and at present nearly all full-time salespeople enjoy the benefits available to other employees.

Every employer is required to pay Social Security taxes on employee earnings. In addition, payments are obligatory for worker's compensation and unemployment compensation. From that point on there are any number of benefits a company can offer its employees. Among them are: pension plans, health and hospital insurance, life and accident insurance, membership in civic or professional associations, contribution for children's education, matching funds for gifts to charitable or educational institutions, and almost everything else you can think of.

No performance qualification is required for eligibility for a fringe benefit although it is usual to establish a waiting period before a new employee is entitled to certain benefits. Some companies absorb the entire cost of such benefits as life and accident insurance while others require the employee to pay part of the cost.

Many companies feel that fringe benefits they provide must be in line with those offered by the competition. I would imagine that few salespeople would seek a job with a particular company only because of the value of the fringes it offered, but they might be reluctant to join a company if they had to pay the major portion of the costs of the few benefits available. They might decide a company niggardly with benefits might also be reluctant to reward good sales production adequately.

Fringe benefits are now a fact of life for all employers. Those expenses are escalating and there appears to be little evidence that the future will see any reduction in either benefits or their cost.

Other Methods of Compensation

From Salesperson's Viewpoint	*From Company's Viewpoint*
DRAWING ACCOUNTS	
Prefer guaranteed to nonguaranteed	Good if business is highly seasonal
Much prefer salary	Effective when used to compensate hires getting started in business
If salary not offered, salespeople, especially new and weaker employee's, welcome draw for the steady income it provides	

Other Methods of Compensation *(continued)*
From Salesperson's Viewpoint   *From Company's Viewpoint*

BONUSES

Discretionary

Too much uncertainity, causes suspicion about method of distribution

1. Problems arise in allocation
2. Can lead to lower morale
3. Controllable expense

Fixed

Prefer fixed bonus, no suprises

1. Excellent incentive when properly used
2. Cost will be determined by sales performance. Projections should be included in expense budget

BONUS-OFFICE

Good for morale of office staff if wisely used

For best results should be based on overall performance of organization

PROFIT-SHARING

Poor substitute for fixed-bonus plan

Unreliable in amount and controlled by overall company profits

As part of compensation plan for salespeople, inferior to bonus as motivator

Good to reward all levels of sales management when accounting system can determine office profits accurately

FRINGES

Generally approve any benefits not too expensive to them

Good benefits may aid in improving sales staff's perception of company

Benefits should be competitive with those of others in industry

Must be concerned with total costs of benefits

Benefits are a tool for improving morale of sales staff and building loyalty

Hints to Sales Managers

- Compare drawing accounts of both types before choosing one, and also compare effectiveness and cost of drawing accounts with salary.
- In setting up a bonus plan, avoid as far as possible the necessity to make subjective judgments.
- Rely on hard data—sales production, new accounts opened, new hires trained.
- But if a salesperson's value to the company also depends on qualitative factors, consider them impartially and equitably.
- Don't forget to include the estimated cost of bonuses in your budget for sales expenses.
- Encourage top management to institute a profit-sharing plan for your office, division or region. It will cost the company, but the return from it should be substantially greater than the expense incurred.
- Analyze competitors' fringe-benefits packages before preparing your own.

CHAPTER 7
Prize Contests

CHAPTER 7

Though a number of salespeople year after year win valuable prizes offered by their employers, it is total compensation package. This is so even though tax laws people require
that the value of most prizes be included in a salesperson's
earnings. Prizes should be considered as an additional fringe
benefit, a perk that rewards superior performance. No responsible sales manager would include the value of prizes in target
earnings figures for members of the staff.

However, like some forms of true compensation, prizes
can provide strong incentives to salespeople to increase their
earnings through extra effort. When well-planned, prize contests, like bonuses, assist companies and their representatives
to attain their goals. Thus it is appropriate for us to consider
the theory and practice of offering contests.

Prize contests are used by a company to stimulate additional sales effort or to direct attention toward specific short-
term company goals. They can be remarkably effective if
designed and handled properly or highly damaging if planning is faulty.

Contests are a fact of life for companies and we'll spend a
few pages on the theory underlying their use as well as comment on the design and promotion of effective contests.

A company can have several reasons for offering a contest:

1. To increase volume of gross sales. This might be a

    long-term objective of a company and the contest would also be long-term in nature—at least three months and perhaps a year.

2. To push special products or overstocked items. Such a goal would be short-term and the contest would also be a short one. Care must be taken to avoid preoccupation with the contest detracting excessively from overall sales objectives.

3. To open new accounts. Such a contest ordinarily would be of short duration.

In general, contests based on important long-range objectives will last longer than those directed at less vital short-term goals. The value of the prizes offered varies with the relative importance of the desired objective. It is not feasible to adjust compensation plans frequently enough to achieve relatively minor goals, and contests are effective means to attain results without disturbing overall compensation policies.

Not every corporation approves of or uses contests to stimulate its employees. They have basic objections to the practice and many are, to an extent, valid.

Contests are habit-forming. Once addicted, withdrawal is difficult. This argument is valid only if the contests are not productive to the company. If they are, why should they be stopped? The salespeople enjoy and profit from stimulating contests and the company also profits. What more could anyone ask?

Development and promotion of a good contest is time-consuming, I agree. So is everything a sales manager does—anything that helps a company and the salesforce is part of the job he or she is paid to do.

Contests based on gross sales volume can cause overselling and slumps before and after the contest. This is certainly true in many industries. For example, a salesperson selling raw steel to a dozen customers has little opportunity to increase overall sales production—manufacturing schedules at factories require just so many tons of steel a month. An increase in orders one month will be deducted from the next month's shipment.

The same argument does not hold true, however, for what I call "creative selling." A house-to-house sales rep selling vacuum cleaners may sell one machine for every four demonstrations made. More demonstrations means more sales and there is no limit to the number of doorbells to be pushed. There must be several million men and women engaged in similar types of selling and the extra effort engendered by a contest puts more money into their pockets and the company coffers.

Another complaint asks why a company should pay a rep twice for doing the same job? The operative word here is "same." If a contest program is properly set up the salesperson won't be doing the same job, but rather doing better than usual—the prize is an extra reward for extra performance. Prizes should be paid like bonuses—on the basis of achievement.

Another objection to contests cites the negative effect on individuals and groups of salespeople who do not win or who know they cannot win as soon as they learn the requirements for winning. The culprit here is not contests in general, but how a particular contest was designed. Prizes offered to one or two top producers will be of no interest to the rest of a salesforce. If a contest requires a single sale for a rep to qualify for a prize and it is awarded by the random selection of one of a hundred entrants, the contest will fail. All contests shouldn't be given a bad rap because a few are poorly set up.

The charge is made that contests are silly kid stuff, beneath the dignity of mature men and women. Well, baseball is a kid's game and each year more than 50 million people enjoy live major league games. And, have you ever seen a $50,000-year sales rep agonizing over a ten-foot side hill putt on the eighteenth green with $2 riding on the outcome? Kid stuff, indeed. I'm all in favor of it.

We've talked enough about poorly organized contests and what they won't do; let's take a look at the other side of the coin. In my opinion a well-designed and -promoted sales contest can be a very strong influence in turning an average salesperson into a star performer. Few salespeople, especially young and inexperienced ones, have any real conception of what they are capable of achieving. Some don't seem to care, being content to crawl along in a comfortable rut. But one out of three or five is ready to explode with the right motivation. That is just what a contest can do.

Consider the situation. A company runs a three-month contest and sales reps who sell seventy-five units in the period are offered their choice among several prizes. A relatively new hire has sold seventeen units in his best month. Among the prizes offered is a shotgun he would give his eye tooth to have, so he buckles down to work and sets out to win it. To his delight he sells seventy-eight units and the gun is his. The prize is important to him, but he has won something infinitely more valuable—knowledge that he is an excellent salesman and confidence in his ability to meet challenges he sets for himself. He worked hard for three months, of course, but now he knows he has the strength to achieve whatever he sets out to accomplish.

The most important benefit of a contest is the effect it can have on a large element of a salesforce. My friend in the example came close to doubling his earnings in the three-month period and the company has reaped a rich harvest of sales. If salesmen are stimulated, the company is bound to profit.

Many "authorities" seem to miss this point entirely. They can see only a temporary spurt in sales that will be reversed in the next month. They ignore the lasting residual effect the contest might have on the lives of a number of its salespeople.

And don't ignore the value of a good example. Others might not have quite the ability and drive of the salesman in our example, but an alert sales manager can capitalize on his or her success to motivate others to succeed as well.

Not long ago, a young woman I know decided to enter a marathon. She had been jogging for some time, but had never run as many as ten miles. Her goal was to finish the twenty-six-mile, 385-yard course and she was determined to do so. I don't know what her doctor would say about the project and I never asked her how long it took her to finish, but finish she did. She'll never run another marathon, that's for sure, but she told me that never again in her life would she doubt her ability to face and conquer any challenge she meets. She tested herself to the extreme, and triumphed.

We never know what we can accomplish until at some point we test ourselves to the utmost. When we do, the result can surprise us. A contest is a good one if it appeals to the imagination of individuals and stimulates them to attempt something they never before believed possible.

In describing the major benefit of an effective contest I have referred only to its impact on the salesforce and said nothing of what it can mean to a company. I don't have to—if a salesforce is stimulated to superior performance, the company can't help but profit in like measure. Don't lose sight of that aspect of contests.

Planning a Major Contest

Let us assume that a company finds its sales volume running behind projections and decides to run a three-month contest expecting to get back on target. For the sake of simplicity we'll also assume the company sells a single major product so the contest will be based on unit sales. For other companies it could, just as easily, be based on total dollar volume of sales.

The first requirement will be to establish a contest cost budget based on the estimated incremental sales the contest will generate. Next a schedule will be made outlining the quotas for winning the various categories of prizes. To it will be added an estimate of the number of winners, the total units they are expected to sell and the cost of the prizes to be awarded in each group.

The schedule on the following page demonstrates this.

So far so good, but now we've got to massage the figures around a bit. First, the cost of $2.20 per unit is a misleading figure. Without the contest, a predictable number of the product would be sold in the normal course of business. The contest cost should be applied against only the incremental sales it generates. The contest planner will check estimates of units to be sold during the contest, subtract normally expected

Prize Category	Number of Units to Win	Number of Winners	Units Sold	Cost of Prizes	Total Cost
A	30	160	4,800	$ 30	$ 4,800
B	45	110	4,950	60	6,600
C	60	60	3,600	100	6,000
D	75	15	1,125	200	3,000
Grand Prizes		2	220	6,000	12,000
Total		347	14,695		$32,400

Cost Per Unit Sold—$2.20

sales and come up with the extra sales the contest should produce. If the contest costs are spread over these sales and the expense per unit is within the contest budget, all is well; if not, cost of prizes must be cut or qualification for winning raised.

In making these estimates the planner will not overlook two important factors. All salespeople will not win a prize, we can be certain of that, but many of the nonwinners will make a valiant effort. Though they fail to reach the minimum number of thirty units, they will sell substantially more than they would have had there been no contest.

In addition, a salesperson who sells the thirtieth unit early in the third month does not take a three-week vacation; he or she shoots for the next category of prize, especially if one of the offerings is something perceived to be really worth winning. Perhaps he or she doesn't reach the magic number of forty-five, but does sell thirty-nine. The extra earnings are welcome solace for the missed goal. Successful contests will generate sales in a variety of ways.

The company's financial officer might well become incensed if expensive trips are to be given to the top two salespeople in the contest. If they sell 100 units each, the cost will be $60 a unit—pure madness. The financial officer has a legitimate concern, but the sales manager thinks differently. He or she knows the value of example, how the success of two salespeople might fire the imagination of a number of others. The manager also knows that any big contest needs one or more equally impressive winners to drive home the message.

What if the cost of the contest goes well above budget? The company will be delighted since the contest will have generated more sales than anticipated. However, should trips be awarded to all those who sold a specified number of units (100 for example) a serious problem could result if twenty individuals met the requirement, against an estimate of two. The lesson to be learned here is that when the units sold can bear the cost of prizes awarded, the more the merrier; but when the cost of the prize far exceeds the contribution of the units sold to win it, care should be exercised to limit total liability.

Should contest costs fall well short of budget, there could be two major causes: either the contest was poorly designed and promoted or winning requirements were set too high.

Types of Prizes

Prizes come in the form of cash, merchandise or travel. Offering cash prizes has several disadvantages. Primarily, there is no discount when buying cash. The cost of $100 is $100. Merchandise can be purchased at discounts ranging up to 50 percent. There is more glamor attached to a $400 watch than to $200 in cash. Furthermore, cash is soon spent and forgotten while a watch can be a life-long reminder of achievement.

Trips are gaining in popularity as prizes, especially when they offer vacations at luxurious resorts or in foreign countries. A fully paid week-long trip to Paris, for a couple, with a room at the Ritz or the Crillon and a chauffeur-driven car at their disposal is enough to turn the head of even the most blasé salesperson.

A variety of prizes should be available in each category. No one item will appeal to everyone and an attempt should be made to cater to as many tastes as possible. Home furnishings or appliances, recreational equipment or tools for hobbyists might be offered; whatever might appeal to a segment of the salesforce.

Qualifications to Win

A contest with only one winner is bad enough, one in which nobody wins is worse. If a prize is awarded to everyone, its value, and it can't be great, is cheapened. The best contests are those that provide an opportunity for everyone to participate with a reasonable chance of winning. That is why four categories of prizes plus the two grand prizes were offered in the example. A goal is set for all types of salespeople: low, medium and high producers. The first level of prizes should be within the reach of every individual, and incentive should increase as each plateau is reached.

You will note that in this contest competition is restricted to the race for the two top prizes. In every other case individuals compete only against themselves. The half dozen at the top can handle rivalry. The losers will lick their wounds and resolve to do better next time. For the present they select the prize they did win and console themselves by figuring how much extra compensation they earned during the contest.

Planning a Minor Group Contest

Assume a company wants to close out a product at a discount. The sales manager decides to run a two-week contest to take care of the situation. He must keep in perspective the relative unimportance of the project and not divert the entire attention of his staff away from their main responsibilities to this minor undertaking. He divides his salesforce into two groups of more or less equal talent. The contest announcement states that at its conclusion a dinner will be held—the winners to eat steak, the losers spaghetti. A capable sales manager with a light touch can get plenty of mileage out of such a contest and the salespeople will enjoy it, too.

Promotion of a Major Contest

Such a program is not to be entered into lightly or without meticulous preparation. It is customary to announce major contests at regional meetings with all salespeople and their spouses as well as sales managers in attendance. The presence of spouses is important. They can be and usually are a potent force in the motivation of their mates.

Color brochures containing photographs of all prizes are distributed. A separate sheet listing requirements to win in each group will also be distributed. Of course, samples of each prize will be unveiled at the gathering, and if furs are offered in the upper categories of prizes, they will be modeled.

If possible, a five-minute color movie showing the marvels of Paris, London or Rome will be run. Airlines and travel agencies make such films available.

Any experienced sales manager knows how to run a meeting of this type: calling on strong producers to pick the prizes they intend to win, asking for a few words from previous trip winners, getting pledges from all levels of salespeople. Note that not one word is said about more sales for the company. The emphasis is on increased earnings for the staff plus the opportunity to win the prize of their choice.

Promotion of the contest continues until the last day. The company house organ lists regional leaders and makes much of the performance of new hires. Personal notes, perhaps only a dozen words in all, flow from all tiers of management. The sales manager spends evenings on the phone encouraging contestants. Short weekly branch meetings keep the pot boiling.

At the conclusion of the contest another regional meeting is held for winners and nonwinners alike. The successful contestants receive their prizes and praise for their achievements; those who didn't win resolve to do better next time.

National Sales Conventions

Many companies hold annual meetings of their salesforces at well-known resorts such as the Boca Raton Club. *Opulent* is the descriptive word. For four or five days, couples live in the lap of luxury, cosseted and catered to as if they were royalty. And royalty they are, for they earned the right to be there. Salespeople must qualify by meeting a production standard during the period since the last national convention or perhaps for a shorter period. Even branch sales managers are often required to earn the trip—a valuable prize. No couple winning it could bear the thought of not returning the following year.

If the contest for an invitation lasts an entire year, new hires, and others due to illness or other causes, will find themselves unable to meet the quota. The company is prepared for this eventuality. At intervals it establishes new quotas for the balance of the year to the point it may set a stiff requirement for the final month. Even a new hire only a few months with the company can earn the right to attend, and that is fitting and proper. The prize is always there, ready to be won until the last possible moment.

Exploitation, critics claim—bribery and constant pressure to produce. Not a bit of it: in the first place, a salesperson with a mind to can turn a deaf ear to what is said about the contest and ignore the bulletins issued on it. Few will.

"Exploitation" is a popular word and it has a very explicit meaning. It is defined as the unjust or improper use of another individual for one's own profit. How far this is from the present situation. Salespeople are encouraged to increase their earnings and they are promised a valuable and attractive bonus if they succeed in doing so—the very opposite of exploitation.

If the salesperson's earning's increase, of course the company profits but it doesn't make an extra dime until the salesperson receives a reward for his or her effort. What could be more fair? It is entirely proper for a company to stimulate and supply incentive to its employees for their own advantage.

Summary

The underlying purpose behind all the preparation and promotion of a contest is to make the sales staff realize their ability and the opportunity they have to break the mental barriers they have set for themselves—to realize they are capable of functioning far more effectively than they ever have in the past. Perhaps a salesperson didn't win even the lowest category prize; yet if the contest was well enough designed that it fired her imagination, she very possibly averaged eight or nine units a month against her previous average of six. No prize, but a 30 percent increase in earnings isn't a bad first step. Next time she will start from a higher level, her horizons will be broadened and her improvement can be even more dramatic when the realization sinks in that she has the power to accomplish whatever goal she sets for herself.

A contest can supply stimulation and offer incentives, but the salesperson requires self-motivation. Few people ever function even close to their full potential. They have no concept of what they can accomplish if they make a conscientious and intelligent effort. It isn't easy to jar a person off dead center. An appealing contest might supply the shove that starts an individual moving in the right direction.

People aspire to better themselves and salespeople are in a preferred position to do so. A sales manager who opens the eyes of the staff to the opportunities awaiting them has given them a precious gift.

The company that regards a contest from the viewpoint of the additional sales it will produce during the weeks or months it runs misses its major value. The residual effect if a mere handful of employees find they can maintain a higher level of productivity can last for years. And think of those who benefit themselves and their families by the new awareness of their capabilities.

Prize Contests

From Salesperson's Viewpoint	*From Company's Viewpoint*
Provide an opportunity to win a prize they would like to have	If well planned and promoted will provide strong stimulation to salesforce
Provide motivation to increase earnings	Will be successful only if they appeal to wide segment of salesforce
Provide useful selling tool—the contest close	The cost can be controlled; the higher the cost of a well-designed plan, the more successful the contest—additional costs are welcome if actual sales exceed projections
If requirements to win too high or prizes not worthwhile, contest will not motivate	
Salespeople like to be winners, to receive praise for accomplishment	Unsuccessful contests damage morale, demotivate salesforce
Top producers will go all out to win the top prize	Anything that increases a sales production and earnings benefits the company
All enjoy the give and take of a well-run minor contest	Consider the possible disadvantages of a contest before running it

Hints to Sales Managers

- Be realistic when planning a contest. Don't give away the farm, but don't set requirements for winning so high that no one wins. The salesforce will be turned off rather than on.
- Make it possible for anyone to win by giving the contest his or her best shot.
- The wider the appeal of a contest the more successful it will be.
- Your primary target is the minds and imagination of your staff. If they are fully motivated and have confidence in their ability to succeed, they will succeed.
- A good contest results in two major benefits: the salesforce is better off and so is the company. One cannot gain without the other being equally successful.
- Running a contest is hard work. Be ready for it.

CHAPTER 8
Compensation Plans

CHAPTER 8

A majority of compensation plans for salespeople combine two or more of the payment methods we have discussed. The most widely used combinations are:

1. Salary plus commission
2. Salary plus bonus
3. Commission plus bonus
4. Salary plus commission plus bonus

Many more variations are possible if we substitute drawing accounts, either guaranteed or nonguaranteed, for salary. And, don't forget incentive prizes used as a source of income for a salesperson, or the value of fringe benefits paid by the employer.

The purpose of a combination plan is to eliminate the weaknesses of individual components and at the same time retain their strengths. The salary element is usually most popular in old, well-established companies that enjoy stable sales. Other companies employing salary as the major element in compensation are those that place heavy emphasis on missionary work, service and other functions not directly connected with sales volume.

More weight is put on the commission component by growing companies concentrating on expanding their business. There, greater incentive is needed and generous commission rates will do much to assure top performance of salespeople.

There has been a recent trend by companies to emphasize incentive over salary. Salaries are escalating in our present economy and employers are becoming increasingly concerned with the rise in fixed costs. On the other hand, there are indications that salespeople, looking for security and stability of income, would welcome a plan that paid half of their income in salary.

When commission is less than 25 percent of total earnings, its incentive effect is vitiated. The reward must be worth the effort or the salesforce will not exert itself to achieve selling potential.

The salary/commission combination is extremely popular, especially when earnings are divided nearly equally between the two. The sales staff has the benefit of security and the company can offer a strong incentive to the sales staff to excel. In addition, if salary is an important part of the compensation package, the company can exert considerable control over the salesman.

If a drawing account of either type replaces salary, a subtle psychological change takes place. The sales staff is grateful for the assured income, yet realizes that it is nothing but an advance on commissions they will earn. They appreciate the loan, but they would prefer salaries they could truly call their own. On the other hand, commission rates are lower if the sales staff is receiving a salary, higher if they receive a draw that will be charged against commissions earned. Thus, the outstandingly productive salesperson who has no problem covering the draw prefers the higher commission rates paid under such a plan.

Whether a draw or a salary is to be paid is a decision each company should analyze before making a choice. The majority of companies use salary instead of drawing accounts when paying fixed compensation to salespeople.

Up to now we have been talking about salary, commission and drawing accounts. Let us see how four equally productive salespeople would fare under various compensation plans. We will assume each has a sales quota of $250,000,

Sales-person	Pay Plan	Salary	Commission	Draw	Total Earnings
A	Salary	$25,000			$25,000
B	10 percent commission		$25,000		25,000
C	$12,500 salary plus 5 percent commission	12,500	12,500		25,000
D	Draw against 10 percent commission		25,000		
		Draw	18,000		
			$ 7,000	$18,000	$25,000

which he or she meets exactly, and an earnings target of $25,000.

As alike as four peas in a pod. It would make no difference financially which method of payment was adopted, either from the salesperson's viewpoint or the company's. We could close our discussion right here if all salespeople could be relied on to do exactly what was expected of them, but that will never happen.

Let us suppose each individual exceeded the sales quota by 10 percent ($25,000) or fell short of it by a like amount. How would earnings be affected?

Salesperson	10 percent above quota	10 percent below quota
A	—0—	—0—
B	$2,500	$(2,500)
C	1,250	(1,250)
D	2,500	(2,500)

What do we learn from these charts? Let's take the salesperson's approach first. The salaried rep receives the same pay whether he sells $225,000, $250,000 or $275,000. If sales have dropped, he worries about a cut in salary next year; if they have increased, he marshals his arguments for asking for a pay rise. Whether his pay is raised or lowered, he is reasonably certain the adjustment, if it is in fact made, will not fully reflect the value of his overage or shortage in sales.

The commissioned rep, B, is pleased when her sales rise; her earnings increase in direct proportion to her production. When the balance tips in the other direction she wonders if she wouldn't have been better off to take half her earnings in salary. Her commission rate would be cut to 5 percent, but when times were bad it would cost her only half of what she lost by remaining on straight commission.

Salesman C, whose earnings are based equally on salary and commission, has the same feelings, but in reverse order. When he sells well above quota he wishes he were on straight commission; when business turns down he is pleased that his stable salary buffers the impact of the loss of commission.

The drawing-account rep, D, has sentiments akin to those of B, the commissioned rep. Whether she is on a guaranteed or nonguaranteed draw will concern her only if her commission earnings fall below the $18,000 draw. If she is on a guaranteed draw, she will not be required to repay the overdraft incurred in a bad year; if the draw is nonguaranteed, the shortage will be recovered from her earnings when they exceed the base of $18,000. Her income, like that of B, the commissioned rep, fluctuates in direct relation to the fluctuation of sales. She does not have the modifying effect of salary to smooth out her earnings.

The company's first concern might be financial—the impact on costs when sales rise or fall. The fixed nature of salaries might be of sizable concern if a drop in sales is deep and prolonged. On the other hand, the increase in commission costs when sales rise should not disturb the company since the added expense would be covered by the income generated by the incremental sales.

I should think the company would be interested in much more than the purely monetary aspects of the rise or fall in the compensation of its salesforce that accompanied similar gyrations in sales. It would question the effectiveness of its compensation plan. Had it been formulated wisely? Was it assisting the company to reach its sales objectives? Were the salepeople adequately and equitably paid? Finally, were the salespeople given the incentive necessary for them to fulfill all the responsibilities of their jobs?

In short, salespeople are concerned primarily with income and security, while the company must take a broader view of the effectiveness of its compensation plan.

When the bonus ingredient is added to a compensation pot, the mixture emits a heady aroma, the faintest whiff of which makes a salesperson's mouth water. The best salespeople are endowed with a strong competitive spirit; set a goal for them and they'll strive to reach it. Offer a valuable prize for success and they will redouble their efforts. Bonuses provide a powerful stimulus to the salesperson's psyche.

It is sometimes difficult for a company paying salaries to develop a basis for a bonus. The company has chosen salary over other methods of compensation for good reasons. We may safely assume other duties than selling are important to it. How then does it measure performance to determine whether a salesperson is worth a bonus?

A point system mightd be the answer. So many points for sales production; so many for each of the other duties an individual is expected to perform. Add up the points and the bonus would reflect the value of the individual's total contribution.

Let's take a look at how such a plan might work. A company could set up a point system, like the one shown on the following page.

The sales manager evaluates performance and allocates points as shown in the second column. The bonus earned would be a percentage of yearly salary according to the following schedule.

Please bear in mind that these figures are not offered as

Job Responsibilty	Point Potential	Salesperson
Sales production	0–12	10
Opening new accounts	0–6	4
Missionary work	0–4	4
Training new hires	0–2	2
Attitude, etc.	0–2	1
Maximum point total	26	21

recommendations in setting up a bonus plan. They are purely illustrative.

Another observation can be made here. The volume of sales written by an individual is a matter of record, so are the number of new accounts opened and the hours spent in the field with recruits. The sales manager is on solid ground when allocating points for performance in these areas, but he or she must rely on subjective judgment when appraising contributions in the other two segments.

When a bonus is combined with commission all salespeople worth the name are happy, provided the potential for substantial reward is present and demands for the attainment of the bonus are not unreasonable. Many companies paying a bonus to commissioned reps base the award solely on sales production. The fact that salespeople are on a straight commission indicates that selling is considered to be their primary responsibility.

As we discussed in a previous chapter, each company has its own method of establishing the amount of the bonus an individual can earn. Some base it on percent of quota achieved, others on total earnings. In either event the amount will be limited by cost considerations and corporate objectives in the sales area.

A combination of salary, commission, and bonus is, from the salesperson's point of view, the best of all possible worlds. He or she has the security of a stable income, the incentive offered by a commission base, and the opportunity to increase income still further by earning a bonus for excelling on the job.

We have emphasized in this chapter the benefits of a fixed bonus rather than a discretionary one. The discretionary type, if used at all, is better suited to fully salaried salespeople than any other class. Salespeople earning at least half their income through commission on sales feel that any bonus paid them should depend on their performance, not the sometimes faulty judgment of executives possibly far removed up the line from them.

Hints to Sales Managers

- When selecting a combination plan, don't confine your analysis to expected results only. What *might* happen is equally important.
- As you analyze keep in mind that your plan should help the company meet its sales objectives. Be sure you know exactly what they are and the effect each component of the plan will have on them.
- Never forget there are two ways to look at a plan: from the company's viewpoint and from the sales-person's. You work for the company, but the salespeople work under your direction—you have an obligation to them as well as to the company.
- The company and the sales staff are not adversaries. A policy benefiting one at the expense of the other is a bad policy. I'll say it again: the company can succeed only through the success of its employees.

CHAPTER 9
Expenses

CHAPTER 9

This is difficult subject to address. There are as many types of expenses as there are salespeople and just as many methods of paying them. As the years pass everything seems to become more complicated and difficult to control. I suppose it's a sign of the times; some people even call it "progress."

I vividly remember the first trip I took at company expense. My round trip in a lower berth was paid for and I was given $10 a day for meals and lodging. The $10 was also expected to cover tips and other incidental expenses. The amazing thing was that it did and I came home a couple of dollars ahead of the game.

But times have changed and so have expense accounts. It is difficult to get a handle on the relationship between corporate expense for salesforce compensation and travel and entertainment costs. The method of compensation used by a company will affect the ratio to a marked extent; so will the company's accounting practices. Some combine all expenses for traveling, by executives as well as the salesforce; others don't. Some companies do not differentiate between inside and outside sales staff, others do.

Salesforce expenses, as distinct from compensation, generally can range anywhere from zero to nearly 40 percent of compensation costs. The "zero" would of course relate to those companies that pay no expenses, and the maximum probably would apply to employers of a small number of

103

high-quality salespeople who travel the world to sell their products or services.

Eliminating the extremes, we can safely suggest that expenses can average between 20 and 30 percent of compensation. Companies are naturally concerned with the magnitude of this cost, but that is by no means the only worrisome issue that confronts them. The Internal Revenue Service is exceedingly strict in its interpretation of what can be classified as a deductible business expense. It takes the attitude that a company can spend its money in any way it wishes provided its stockholders approve, but travel and entertainment costs must conform to established guidelines before they can be deducted on income tax returns.

Regulations cover not only the classification of items that are or are not acceptable as deductions, but also detail the documentation necessary to validate them. Thus, evidence must be presented to demonstrate not only that the expense is of a type and amount allowed, but also that proper receipts prove the money was actually spent.

As a result, companies employing a number of men and women on expense accounts must maintain voluminous and precise records. Individuals must secure receipts and attach them to expense reports submitted to employers for reimbursement. Companies not only have to audit them for accuracy and compliance with company policy, but also to assure that expenses will meet government requirements for deductibility. In addition close watch must be kept on changes in the regulations that affect either the acceptability or validation of expenses.

Thus, when a company reimburses salespeople's expenses it must provide an auditing and accounting staff as well as a legal expert in order to protect its interests. The result is a further increase in costs.

If a company requires its representatives to pay their own expenses it escapes these responsibilities, transferring them to the individuals involved. The general rule is that the party claiming the expense deduction is responsible for adherence to government requirements with respect to deductibility and validation of expenses. This point will come up again and again as we discuss the major options available to a company in handling the travel and entertainment expenses of its salesforce.

We'll start by listing a few of the major types of expenses normally incurred by salespeople.

1. Travel—usually by air or car
2. Meals
3. Lodging
4. Entertainment
5. Miscellaneous

Before we go into a discussion of these costs we should talk a little about the types of salespeople that incur them. It is a fact of life that all salespeople are not equal. Some highly educated and trained people earn well in excess of $100,000 a year. Others, just as worthy in their way, drive trucks delivering their products daily to dozens of retail outlets. That is the economic side of the equation.

One breed of sales reps criss-cross the country a dozen times a year, calling on top executives wherever they go. Others find their sales in a six-square-block area of Manhattan. Geography plays a major part in determining the amount of expense money they will spend.

So does the social environment in which the individual operates. For one, a couple of beers at Clancy's Bar will suffice to maintain a friendly relationship with a customer; for another, haute cuisine and vintage wines at the Plaza are *de riguer*.

The method of compensation also plays a role in the handling of expenses. As a general rule, the employer of salaried salespeople is usually responsible for all the business expenses of its staff. Salespeople on straight commission customarily pay their expenses out of generous commission rates. Various plans are used when compensation combines salary and commission.

Missionary reps paid by salary usually receive a fixed expense allowance or the company picks up all the tabs. Here I refer to the man or woman who delivers breakfast cereals and racks the boxes in the supermarket, the actual order having been written by a sales executive at the buying office of the chain.

At this point we'll examine in some detail the most widely used methods of handling sales expenses.

Expenses Paid by Salespeople

When a sales rep pays his or her own expenses it is unnecessary for the company to maintain any records, nor does its auditor have to check the amount or legitimacy of an expenditure. The result is a substantial saving for a company employing a number of reps, but this method of handling expenses is not an unmixed blessing to the employer.

Commission rates must be increased by an amount sufficient to cover the individual's costs. This is not as easy as it sounds. Costs of food and lodging vary in different parts of the country and fluctuate even in adjacent territories. One rep with a small compact area to cover is home every night and drives no more than 10,000 miles a year calling on customers. Another sleeps away from home three or four nights a week and drives 40,000 miles a year in covering the territory. The company cannot have a different commission schedule for everyone, so an arbitrary adjustment is made in rates. Some will profit, others may lose, but what else can be done?

A further complication results when sales fluctuate. In good times not all the rate increase is devoted to paying expenses; the salesperson profits, at times substantially. Conversely, when a salesperson's production falls for any of a number of reasons, he or she is reluctant to spend money on any but essential expenses and is inclined to cut out entertaining that might be important to the company—in short, skimpy in any way possible. The individual might even decide not to make trips that should be made. A further decrease in sales costs the salesperson as much as the company, but that is what people will do to save a few dollars.

By losing control of expense money the company also loses control over the spending habits of its reps. Staid and prestigious companies do not approve when their representatives stay at third- or fourth-rate motels and drive around in eight-year-old, battered heaps.

How do salespeople regard a policy under which they pay their expenses? In the first place the necessity of maintaining exact records is transferred to them. In order to deduct business expenses, they must satisfy the Internal Revenue Service that the money was actually spent and that it was spent for purposes allowed by the regulations. Furthermore they must be able to produce evidence in the form of receipts to verify expenditures. Some reps will attempt to beat the system, but should a day of reckoning arrive, the salesperson will have more pressing duties than selling the company's products until the misunderstanding is cleared up.

It is safe to say that reps will be more conservative spending their own money than if it is company largesse they are dispensing.

So much for reps who pay their own expenses. We'll now shift to the other end of the spectrum—the rep whose expenses are fully paid by the company.

Expenses Paid by Company

Travel

First of all, the salesperson must understand exactly what expenses the employer deems proper. On plane trips a company might permit travel only at coach rate. Reps of higher status might be permitted to enjoy business-class accommodations, and even first class if they are home office moguls. Whatever the rules are on air travel, they must be made clear to the sales staff.

The same is true for lodging. Many companies establish allowable rate levels for different areas of the country. A room in downtown Chicago costs more than one in Florence, South

Carolina. For that matter, so does a meal. In many parts of the country a guideline of $25 a day for meals would allow a rep to eat like a king, but a rep in New York might easily exceed this limit by lunchtime.

Other Expenses

Let's assume the company reaches an understanding with its sales staff on travel, lodging and meals. How about other necessary expenses like laundry and valet services? The prevalent theory is that the salesperson should expect the company to pay all expenses that would not incur provided he or she was at home. In any case, laundry must be cleaned and pressed. Some companies authorize laundry and cleaning expenses only if a rep is away for a week or more. Others, more graciously, allow them at all times.

What about a taxi from the airport into town instead of the shuttle bus? Whatever the company policy, it should be clearly understood by the sales staff.

May a rep phone home in the evening to learn if the furnace or the air conditioner has been repaired or to find how Linda did on the spelling test? I should hope so, but let company policy be a matter of record.

The general rule is that a person should be able to continue his or her normal living habits while traveling on an expense account. The standard should be neither above nor below what the individual is accustomed to at home. That is a good rule that should be agreeable to both the company and the sales staff.

How about entertaining? The company expects a certain amount of it from its reps. Dinner and theater tickets can cost a small fortune, but being too cheap can cost even more in customer relations. Judgment is the key and company policy should establish guidelines.

A word about recordkeeping. Companies have forms for recording expenses if they have more than one or two individuals on expense accounts. Reports must be presented to the company before reimbursement is made. That is one report salespeople are not reluctant to prepare.

The reports must be checked to see if the arithmetic passes muster, but also to determine if expenditures are for authorized purposes and are not excessive in amount. In addition, receipts will be reviewed to determine if they conform with government requirements that will make them acceptable as deductible company expenses.

At times it is difficult for a rep to personally finance a lengthy trip. Many companies authorize a permanent advance to a rep that will be reimbursed when the rep's expense account is approved. If a rep handles this money through a personal checking account there is always the possibility that company funds will at times be devoted to other uses than those intended.

Bear this in mind: control does not connote stinginess. It does imply that company policies are to be followed, that unauthorized expenditures will not be honored and that padding will be detected and dealt with. Well-adjusted reps content with their jobs and their compensation are not overly inclined to juggle their expense accounts.

What effect does payment of all traveling expenses have on a company? It makes it difficult to control selling expenses or even to budget for them accurately. Perhaps knowing that the company will pick up the tab begets an extravagant attitude on the part of salespeople who have no incentive to economize. Finally, the office staff and the sales manager must have sharp eyes to police expense accounts and to spot seemingly unnecessary trips to the scene of the World Series.

Interestingly, company policies on expenses are more often too liberal rather than too tough. The reason is that companies know the effect on sales when they are constantly feuding, at times acrimoniously, with reps about questionable expense account items.

Salespeople are relieved that their responsibility mends when the company accepts their expense accounts. If the tax collector has a complaint, the dispute is between him and the company, not the salesperson. The rep also enjoys a sense of security: expenses are not controlled by sales volume, and he or she cannot be made responsible for any expenditures provided they were consistent with company policy.

The company finds recordkeeping and auditing expensive. Also, sales expenses fall into the fixed classification—they maintain their constant course whether sales rise or fall. This is a disadvantage to a company in slack periods.

On the plus side, the company can control the activities of its reps. It knows where they have been, and what they were doing, which would not have been the case if they paid their own expenses and went where they pleased. When a company pays a rep's expenses, his or her earnings are not affected and payroll deductions and taxes are not involved. The expense is handled like any other profit-and-loss item on the company's statement.

Fixed Expense Allowance

Under this plan the company avoids the recordkeeping and auditing required when it pays a representative's expenses. Consider it this way: when a company reimburses expenses, it assumes the responsibility of justifying them to state or federal government auditors. They are the company's expenses, not the salesperson's. When the company does not reimburse expenses directly, the salesperson is responsible for validating them on tax returns.

Under a fixed expense-allowance plan, the company pays a rep an agreed amount for each day, week or month to cover the expected expenses. The allowance paid is added to the rep's earnings and necessary deductions are taken from it. The rep then claims the actual expenses as deductions on tax returns. The allowance might vary from $10 a day to $5,000 or more a month and a check will be issued at designated intervals.

This plan has many similarities to that under which a commissioned rep is paid at a higher rate and is responsible for expenses. The only real difference is that under the allowance method the rep receives a fixed sum hand-tailored to his or her needs, rather than a higher return on sales. The added commission a rep receives, depending as it does on sales volume, is a variable expense to the company. A continuing allowance is a fixed expense, not affected by fluctuations in sales.

Let's see how a fixed-allowance plan might work.

Sales Rep	Days Away	Lodging ($65/night)	Meals ($50/day)	Lunch ($10)	Misc.	Total
A	3	$195	$150	$20	$40	$375
B	1	65	80	30	90	$265

Sales Rep A has a widespread territory and his regular schedule requires him to be away from home three nights a week. He can get a room in a first-class motel for $65 a night. His food allowance of $50 a day while he is away will allow him to eat well and even have a drink before dinner. The company generously allows him $10 for lunch on the days he will return home at night. Some employers might feel that when the man leaves home for work and returns in time for dinner he is no different from the ordinary office worker who buys lunch every day. Who can deny the equity of their attitude? Yet, this company includes two lunches in the allocation.

Sales Rep A is not expected to entertain customers in the normal course of his activity, so he receives $40 weekly for miscellaneous expenses such as tolls, parking and the like. On special occasions when he finds it necessary to entertain, he submits a receipt for the expense and hopes to receive reimbursement.

Sales Rep B has a different-sized territory which requires her to be away only a single night a week. On the other hand, her customers are such that she does receive a regular allocation for entertaining.

You will note that up to this point we have said nothing about automobile expenses. They have not been forgotten: they are so important we will devote a special section of the chapter to them.

A fixed expense allowance is good for a company provided sales management is firmly in control of the salesforce. Allowances must be set only after a full study has been made of the travel pattern of each rep and the varying costs of food and lodging in each territory. The activities of all reps must be closely monitored: are they actually doing what their schedules call for, making the trips they are scheduled to make? Managers must be alert to changes and make timely adjustments in allowances when necessary.

Under this method of expense reimbursement a salesperson may be reluctant to seek new accounts located at a distance from one of his or her regular stops, might even attempt to increase income by using the telephone rather than calling on a distant customer.

The company's workload is reduced in recordkeeping and auditing. Whether selling expenses will be higher or lower and more or less effectively utilized than they would be under another method of payment depends on the ability of the sales manager to set allowances accurately on his or her complete knowledge of what the staff is actually doing in the field.

Expense Allowances Based on Sales

Companies may employ another means of making an expense allowance by which a rep would receive 3 or 4 percent of his or her total sales amount to cover expenses. This method offers two major advantages to an employer. It relieves the company of the necessity of maintaining any expense account records since the allowance is added to the rep's earnings and it is the rep's responsibility to validate deductions. Secondly, selling expenses become a variable expense rather than a fixed charge. The company pays a rep a percentage of gross sales it can afford and as far as it is concerned, that is the end of the matter.

Some salespeople will make a substantial profit out of such a deal; others might have to dig into their own pockets if their particular selling expenses are high. To be as equitable as possible the company should set a rate for each salesperson or perhaps each class of salespeople, but this is seldom if ever possible. Many variables make successful solutions to inherent problems difficult to achieve. One rep sells high-volume, low-margin products; another low-volume, high-margin ones. The rep in one territory might sell 90 percent of his or her business to a handful of customers located within an hour's drive of home. Another must spend all week on the road to get modest orders from dozens of accounts.

Inequities are inevitable under this system. The amount of expense allowance is made purely a function of sales volume, but actual expenses incurred might be controlled by a half-dozen other factors, all more relevant than sales.

Combination Plans

It is not unusual for a company to pay actual costs of travel and lodging and make a fixed allowance for meals and other expenses. The company's recordkeeping is confined to plane tickets and hotel or motel costs. Both are easy to document. The salesperson takes care of all other evidences of payment. The establishment of the amount of the fixed allowance follows the procedure already outlined.

Another method often used to reimburse salespeople for expenses other than traveling costs sets one per diem rate for reps at home and another when they are on the road. Such a system eliminates much of the inequity involved in a fixed-rate allowance plan under which a salesperson receives an amount based on estimates of where his or her time will be spent.

Per diems will vary with local prices. In one area $100 will cover lodging, meals and miscellaneous charges adequately; in another it might not be sufficient. A per diem plan will allow the company to exert some amount of control over expenses and the activities of its reps.

A rep working his or her home area might be allowed $10 a day for incidentals. Entertainment costs can be built into a per diem, but if the company so elects it can require its salespeople to list their entertainment costs on a special report. Under this system the company has greater control over the expenses.

Summary

Before we turn to automobile expenses and how they can be handled, we'll add a chart covering the pros and cons from the sales staff's and company's viewpoints of the various methods of paying expenses that we have discussed.

Payment of Expenses

From Sales Staff's Viewpoint	*From Company's Viewpoint*
	SALESPERSON PAYS
Records are required to support expense deductions on tax records	No records required
	Higher commission rate is a variable expense
More money is available in good times, less in bad; yet expenses continue on an almost even keel	Little control over reps' comings and goings possible
	Plan does not differentiate between costs in various territories
It is possible to skimp on standards of living when away from home and thereby increase disposable income	The plan cannot be equitable to all reps
Some reps profit from increased commission rates and some lose out depending on travel demands of different territories	Clear-cut company policy is essential, covering allowable expenses; similar precise explanation of acceptable limits for food, lodging and so forth is necessary; policies should reflect full understanding of costs throughout the area
No records need be kept by salespeople other than those required to secure reimbursement from company	
An extravagant attitude may develop in minds of salespeople	Voluminous and exact records must be kept; expense reports must be examined to prevent padding or inclusion of unauthorized items

---

Payment of Expenses *(continued)*

From Sales Staff's Viewpoint   *From Company's Viewpoint*

EXPENSES PAID BY COMPANY

The company has diminished control over sales staffs' expenses as long as they conform with company policy

The company has greater control over the activities of its reps as it has a full record of their travels and calls

EXPENSE ALLOWANCE BASED ON SALES

From Sales Staff's Viewpoint	*From Company's Viewpoint*
Salespeople must keep records for tax purposes	No recordkeeping or auditing required
Plan is not equitable to all reps; some territories are more or less expensive to cover than others	Expenses are variable, not fixed
	Plan bases allowance on sales, which may have little to do with actual expenses
	Does not differentiate between high-volume, low-margin and low-volume, high-margin sales

COMBINATION PLANS

Company pays travel and lodging, salesperson receives fixed allowance for other expenses

From Sales Staff's Viewpoint	*From Company's Viewpoint*
Salesperson must keep records for tax purposes	Company must keep tax records, although to a lesser extent
Salesperson cannot spend a week at home phoning customers without company's knowledge; this would have been possible under a fixed allowance plan	Makes fixed allowance much simpler to figure, yet problems of equity remain
	Expenses are semi-controllable
	Company does know where reps have or have not been

Payment of Expenses (continued)

From Sales Staff's Viewpoint   *From Company's Viewpoint*
COMBINATION PLANS

*Company pays travel and sets per diem amount
for other expenses*

Salesperson must keep records   Company recordkeeping
More equitable than fixed-allow-   minimal
  ance plan as it is more closely   Per diem allowance is more
  tied to rep's activities   accurate than fixed-allowance
    plan
    Company has greater knowl-
    edge of salesforce activity and
    can exert greater control over
    it

Automobile Expenses

Three categories of cars are used by salespeople: company-owned, rented, and salesperson-owned. We'll discuss each in order.

Company-Owned Cars

The company buys a car, secures license plates, pays the insurance premiums and property taxes and turns the car over to a salesperson. When the car has outlived its usefulness the company disposes of it and buys another. While the salesperson has it the company pays for gas, oil, tires, maintenance and repairs when needed.

The company keeps depreciation records on each car and when it is ultimately sold either a profit or a loss is booked on the transaction. Company expenses fall into two groups: fixed and variable. Once the depreciation is set up it is a fixed expense; so are insurance, property taxes and license fees. Such costs are paid even if the car is never used.

Variable expenses include gas, oil, tires, maintenance and so forth, all of which are controlled by the number of miles the car is driven. Many companies replace cars after three years or 60,000 miles, whichever comes first.

Let's take a look at this from the company's point of view. Recordkeeping is voluminous and costly. Individual records are kept on each vehicle, and if a company has a large fleet, a division must be created in the accounting department to handle them. The purchase cost of cars is held down by discounts available to fleet buyers.

It would be a mistake not to mention the investment angle with regard to company-owned cars. A company needs substantial resources to buy 100 or 1,000 cars. Of course they aren't all bought at the same time; a fleet turns over about 30 percent a year. Still, fifty cars cost a small fortune. (Have you bought even one lately?)

How does a company determine whether it gets its money's worth out of a car it supplies to a salesperson? First let's estimate the annual fixed costs. If a car will be depreciated over three years and add the other fixed costs, we find the annual fixed expense can reach $3,000 to $6,000. Of course, the make and model of the cars purchased will have a major effect on this total, as will the area of the country where they are registered. For the sake of simplicity we'll use the figure of $5,000 for our example. The costs of operating the car will probably average around twenty-five cents a mile.

If a salesperson drives the car 10,000 miles, the cost to the company is fifty cents a mile for fixed costs plus twenty-five cents for variable ones, a total of seventy-five cents a mile. At 20,000 miles the total would be fifty cents a mile—twenty-five cents fixed plus twenty-five cents variable. At 30,000 miles the total costs would drop to forty-one cents.

A company would be prudent to prepare a chart using the appropriate figures and compare it to the results that it would obtain should the company rent its cars or require salespeople to provide their own. We'll do this later in the chapter.

We can say that the more mileage a salesperson puts on a company car, the more economical it will be for the company to own it. How the costs will compare with other types of ownership needs to be determined before a company decides how to handle transportation of its salesforce. So much for the financial side.

The company can choose the make and model of the cars it provides for its staff. It can arrange for a distinctive paint job on its cars and even for advertising on the body if it wishes. The company, if it is concerned with the image it wishes to project, can control the age and appearance of the cars used by its reps.

Salespeople like driving company-owned cars. They don't have to worry about any of the costs of ownership—putting out their own funds and then hoping to get a square deal from the company. Having someone else totally responsible is comforting.

Rented Cars

Companies renting cars avoid much of the recordkeeping that goes along with ownership. Makes and models can be selected, used as long as desired and then returned to the renter with no need to dispose of the discards. The company also escapes the requirement to pay large sums to buy cars.

Rental companies are in business to make money—don't ignore that fact. They must do all the clerical work a company would have to do if it owned the cars; they have to buy and pay for the cars they rent. Rental rates are set high enough to cover costs and return a profit. Thus it would appear that paying rent on its fleet would be more expensive to a company than owning it. Yet many companies are content to pay the premium to avoid the large investment and the administrative requirements that accompany ownership.

It makes no difference to a salesperson whether the car is rented or company-owned. As long as the rep doesn't have to pay for the car, he or she doesn't care who does.

Salesperson-Owned Cars

We have already determined that it is not economical for a

company to buy or rent cars for a group of salespeople who will not use them extensively. Owning or renting cars is good business for a company when the staff puts high mileage on them, bad business when mileage is low.

When the car is owned by the salesperson the company has no control over either its age or appearance. Some salespeople are proud of their cars and keep them in tip-top condition; to others a car is merely a means of transportation and it suits them as long as it runs.

A salesperson's principal worry is whether the company will provide a car allowance sufficient to cover operating costs with enough remaining to buy a new car to replace one near the end of its useful life. If the allowance is generous, an economy-minded rep might cover expenses and have a little cushion left. If it is on the stingy side, the rep will be resentful.

Now we'll consider how a company can reimburse its reps driving company or rented cars for gas and normal upkeep charges, and make equitable payment to those using personal cars on company business.

Reimbursement for Car Expenses

The simplest plan—and the easiest to administer—a company can adopt is to pay one fixed mileage rate on cars it owns or rents and a higher fixed rate to reps who drive their own cars. Unfortunately, simplicity is not necessarily a synonym for equity.

Maintenance costs vary in different parts of the country. More antifreeze is sold in Minnesota than Florida; brakes wear out quicker in San Francisco than in Kansas; many snow tires are sold in Maine, but few in Louisiana. Even the price of gasoline differs substantially in different areas.

The variation in costs is even wider when we consider fixed costs such as the insurance and property taxes a salesperson must pay if driving a car on company business. Liability, casualty and property damage rates can double from one area to another. Property taxes are shockingly high in some states, minimal in others.

A company owning or renting cars usually reimburses

salespeople for all normal maintenance and operating costs. Since gas and oil are included in this category the salesperson presents receipts and is reimbursed. Many reps carry a company credit card and the bills are submitted directly to the company. The theory is simple—when the company supplies the car, the company picks up all the bills. No problem there.

If the salesperson owns the car, there are a number of ways to pay his or her expenses, as we next condiser.

Payment Based on Mileage. A company may pay reps thirty cents a mile to compensate them for the using their cars. Such a payment presents no administrative problems to the employer. The reps list the mileage for each trip they make and the company pays them. Salespeople who do extensive business driving—30,000 miles or more a year—like this system of reimbursement. The reason is clear—they make money. Actual operating costs average around fifteen cents a mile, leaving fifteen cents a mile to pay fixed charges. Thus, if a rep drives 30,000 miles, he receives $4,500 toward these expenses which, depending on what make and model car he drives, might not exceed $3,500. On the other hand, the salesperson who drives only 10,000 miles on company business would receive only $1,500 to cover fixed costs, and would be left deep in a hole.

Salespeople know what they are going to receive. They might not like it but at least they know. Companies are able to estimate closely the payments they will make, so budgeting problems are reduced.

The major weakness of this method of reimbursing salespeople is that it is inequitable.

Fixed-Sum Payment Plus Mileage. This method avoids the weakness of the straight-mileage plan. Under it a salesperson receives a fixed amount each month—$300 for example—plus fifteen cents per mile driven. Each rep is thus assured of $3,600 a year to cover fixed costs. The mileage allowance should take care of normal operating expenses.

But what about the rep who uses a car only occasionally on company business and at least half of its annual mileage is attributable to family use? In such cases the company would reduce the fixed allowance to $150 a month and mileage would be paid only for the distance covered while on company business.

In this connection, we might mention that companies are usually generous in permitting reasonable personal use of company-owned or rented vehicles that are driven extensively on company business. More often than not they pay all operating and maintenance expenses, even though the salesperson may put 1,000 miles or so on the car each year dropping the children off at school or doing the grocery shopping. Expenses incurred while on extended vacation trips might be handled differently.

Sliding Scale Mileage Rates. This method seeks to achieve results similar to those obtained from a fixed allowance plus mileage plan. A salesperson might be paid thirty cents a mile for the first 12,000 miles, twenty-two cents on the next 12,000, and seventeen cents on the excess over 24,000 miles. If this individual drove 30,000 miles in a year, the payment would work out like this:

First	12,000	miles at 30¢	=	$3,600
Next	12,000	miles at 22¢	=	2,640
Final	6,000	miles at 17¢	=	1,020
Total	30,000			$7,260
Operating expenses at 15¢				4,500
Contribution to fixed charges				$2,760

Results are satisfactory to a salesperson who drives 30,000 miles a year. If the territory was such that the rep need put only 15,000 miles on the odometer, he or she would receive $2,010 to cover fixed costs.

It must be recognized that when we use $3,600 as an estimate of fixed costs and fifteen cents a mile as an operating expense figure we do not expect you to consider them as anything but extremely rough guidelines. Actual figures will vary with the make and model of the cars involved, the fluctuations in the cost of gas and tires, the replacement costs of automobiles and the cost of insurance needed to cover the owners of the cars.

There is no single "best" way to reimburse a salesperson for the use of his or her car on company business. Some companies avoid the problem by simply increasing commission rates and telling salespeople to provide their own transportation. A cop-out? Perhaps, but think of the recordkeeping and auditing a company avoids, the hassles it escapes with reps who are dissatisfied with their allowances. Of course, a lot would depend on the commission or salary adjustment. If a salesperson's total compensation, after deducting for car expenses, is competitive and adequately rewards productivity, neither the salesperson nor the company should have any basis for complaint.

The accompanying graph projects company costs under several methods of handling car expense. We are staying with our choices of $3,600 fixed expense and twenty cents a mile variable cost. Rental costs are not included; we assume they would at least equal and probably exceed the $3,600 figure. It is hoped that managers able to secure actual company costs can tailor the graph to the actual conditions in their company and the adjusted chart would indicate in what direction they should proceed.

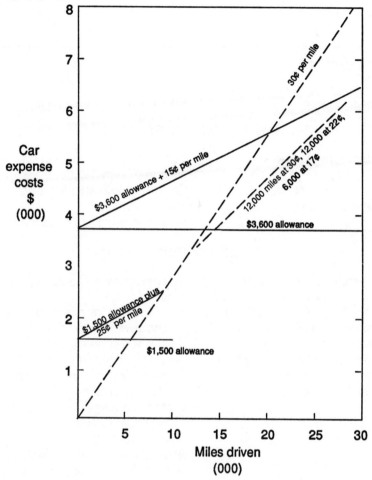

Payment Schedule	10,000 Miles	20,000 Miles	30,000 Miles
30¢ per mile	$3,000	$6,000	$9,000
$3,600 fixed plus 15¢ per mile	5,100	6,600	8,100
30¢ first 12,000 miles 22¢ next 12,000 miles 17¢ additional 6,000 miles	3,000	4,760	7,260
$1,500 fixed plus 25¢ per mile	4,000	N/A	N/A

Car Expenses

From Salesperson's Viewpoint   *From Company's Viewpoint*

OWNED OR RENTED CARS

Salesperson pleased when com-   Company controls age and con-
  pany pays all expenses   dition of cars
  and will replace car   Company obligated for large
  when required   fixed expenses
                                    Administrative expenses high

SALESPERSON-OWNED CARS

High-mileage salespeople   No control over age and appear-
  prefer flat mileage rate   ance of cars
Low-mileage reps prefer fixed   Fixed mileage rate is easiest to
  allowance plus mileage to   administer, but excessively
  cover operating expenses   costly when mileage is high
All approve sliding scale mile-   Option of increasing salary or
  age rates, provided they   commission rate to cover car
  are adequate   costs is alternative
                                   Costs are easier to calculate and
                                     forecast; administrative costs
                                     are minimized
                                   Fixed allowance plus mileage is
                                     equitable and cost efficient

Hints to Sales Managers

- Whatever plan you adopt to cover sales expenses, make sure it is thoroughly understood by your staff.
- Be familiar with the travel routines of your staff. Determine what lodging and meals cost throughout your territory.
- Don't be a miser, but don't make yourself an easy mark for your salesforce.
- Get in the habit of checking where your reps are going by studying their expense reports.
- Is your expense policy more or less liberal than those of leading competitors? If so, why?
- Analyze your company's car expense policy. Are some individuals treated better than others? Can the imbalance be corrected?

CHAPTER 10
Territories

CHAPTER 10

W e have taken a good look at the factors that can be used to build a compensation base (salary drawing accounts commissions, bonuses) and have seen how reimbursement of expenses can fit in. Other areas must be discussed before we go about setting up a sample compensation plan. The first of these is territories.

I have no idea where or when the territorial concept had its beginnings—for humans, that is. Animals have always staked their claim to an area of ground; man has developed similar tendencies throughout the millenia since the cave dwellers flourished.

When the historical era dawned, who were the first itinerant merchants to peddle their wares throughout a region they claimed as their private domain? Where did they ply their trade?

Perhaps it was in Greece when men of prodigious memory went from village to village reciting the immortal verses of Homer to rapt audiences; perhaps it was in medieval Europe when the *jongleur*, the wandering minstrel, sang and recited the story of Roland in the castles of the nobility.

Perhaps in a more modern time it was the Yankee peddler tramping with heavy pack through the scattered settlements of the colonies, or his grandson following the sun in a loaded wagon drawn by a team of patient horses or oxen. Each of these individuals probably followed the same beaten track from year to year, seeing the same villages, castles or customers and building their clientele as they traveled. In even more modern times appear the Willy Lomans of commerce, laden down with heavy sample cases, offering their wares to buyers throughout their territories.

In passing, I urge all sales managers, experienced old hands and neophytes just appointed, to read or reread Arthur Miller's classic drama *Death of a Salesman*. Its insights into the life of a traveling salesman have a shattering effect on a reader: the triumphs of the old days, the desolation and defeats as Willy ages and loses his confidence, his unanswered plea for a salary, any salary, when he can no longer earn a commission sufficient to support his wife and himself. It confronts us with the reality of the world of selling.

Willy Loman to his wife, Linda:

"Cause I get so lonely—especially when business is bad and there's nobody to talk to. I get the feeling that I'll never sell anything again, that I won't be making a living for you or a business, a business for the boys."

Further along, Linda says:

"A small man can be just as exhausted as a great man. He works for a company thirty-six years this March, opens up unheard of territories to their trademark, and now in his old age they take his salary away." [1]

Selling is a tough game; don't let anyone ever tell you different. Willy was not a great salesman by any standard even though he was proud he averaged $170 a week in 1928. Yet he always did his best to the extent of his ability, despite his mistakes and weaknesses. He deserved a better fate. Read Willy's story and profit from the experience.

Many companies learned early on that it was necessary to establish clearly defined territories, not only for district offices but also for individual salespeople. Yet, this is not universally so. To a number of industries a wide-open policy is not only preferable but essential. Insurance agents, mutual-fund representatives, real estate brokers and agents, and other personal service organizations could not function effectively if strict

---

[1] Copyright 1979 by Arthur Miller, Permission of International Creative Management, Inc.

territorial limits were enforced. Personal relationships are a paramount importance in those professions, and such relationships know no geographical boundaries. Thus a man or woman in such a business must be free to sell wherever customers can be found. It is also true that in the high-tech industries the individual best qualified to handle a specific account is assigned to it regardless of where the account is located.

No substantial administrative problems should be encountered when a territory is considered open to all the representatives operating in it. If a lead is received, the manager gives it to the next name on the list. Bad feelings can develop if the manager shows favoritism in passing out leads or, what is worse, claims office sales as his or her own; but a person who would do that probably has other failings as well and won't be around very long.

Despite the exceptions noted, the vast majority of companies do find the territorial concept the best approach to the marketing function. Districts are established and reps assigned to well-defined segments of them. Ordinarily they have exclusive rights to all sales made in their territory.

It is inevitable that as time goes on territories, as well as personnel, change. Furthermore, territorial boundaries must be fixed when a company expands into a new area. Thus, organization and reorganization of territories is an ongoing function of sales management and an understanding of these two functions is required when establishing or modifying compensation plans in areas where territories are being restructured. Consequently, we'll devote a few pages to this subject.

Territory Evaluation

When we consider the word *territory* we usually think in terms of geography. "Northwest Territory" has a romantic ring to it, as does "Yukon Territory." Towering firs and broad rivers in one, snow-capped mountains and rivers of ice in the other.

In a selling sense territory means something quite different. The sales executive thinks in terms of people, customers to whom goods or services can be sold, rather than areas on a map. Geography, however, cannot be ignored. Potential customers are not herded together in a convenient bundle waiting for a salesperson to descend on them. They are scattered across the map and if the sales manager is to make them profitable customers, he or she must find an economic way to get salespeople inside their purchasing departments.

Some territories are like abandoned gold mines. Chemical analysis has disclosed that gold is present, but the cost of extraction is greater than the value of the gold extracted. Similarly, the trick is to secure sales at a cost low enough to assure that a profit can be made from them.

There are many information sources available to a company seeking to decide whether it might be profitable to move into a new area. Government publications are available containing statistical information on over 500 basic trading areas and 50 major ones. More than 300 metropolitan areas are surveyed. There are over 3,000 counties in the country and information is available for each one of them. Chambers of Commerce are always ready to supply information on factories and wholesale or retail establishments located in the area. Municipal and county governments can be helpful along the same line.

A company wishing to expand will examine the information it accumulates and pick an area that looks promising. If it is cautious, it will take a number of steps before sending in two or three reps and preparing to handle the flood of orders they are expected to produce. The more it knows about a territory the better its chance for a successful expansion. Let us list a number of the points a sales manager would consider in deciding whether it would pay to expand into a particular area:

1. The number of possible customers in the area. Break them down into classifications: large, medium-sized, small.

2. The location of possible customers. Are they concentrated in one or more clearly defined locations, or scattered through the area?
3. The potential value of the entire market in the area.
4. The caliber of the competition that will be encountered. How many competitors are there? What is the quality of their products or services? What is a realistic assessment of your chances of enticing customers away from them?
5. The share of market you should be able to achieve and how long it will take to attain it.
6. The workload required to cover the territory. The sales manager makes a preliminary route schedule for covering the territory. He or she has already gotten a fix on the number of prospects to be called on, broken them down into those where one call a month will suffice, others to be called on twice a month, and a few that should be visited every week. This list determines the number of calls to be made each month. The sales manager already knows company standards for average time spent on calls, so total time is easily computed. Travel time is roughly estimated from the routes that have been sketched out, added to call time, and a total is arrived at. It is quickly apparent how many reps will be required to cover the territory. Perhaps the study reveals that three reps are needed. Undaunted, the sales manager passes along to the final point.
7. Comparison of costs of manning the territory with sales to be expected from it. Three reps, let us say, will cost the company $120,000 a year in compensation plus an additional $35,000 for expenses. It is not to be expected that sales in the first year, at least, will be of sufficient volume to cover this substantial investment. The sales manager refers back to the market estimates prepared previously (see number 5) and compares it with projected costs. Is the risk of going in with three reps worth taking, or would it be

more prudent to start with a single rep covering a much smaller and more concentrated group of potential customers? If that were done and the rep proved successful, coverage could be expanded by assignment of one or more trainees to the area at a later date.

The sales manager decides, calls the boss at the home office and shares the results of the study and asks for (and usually receives) authority to proceed as proposed. Let us hope the manager's decision is sound. It will be, provided the analysis was thorough and the estimates reasonably attainable.

Opening New Territories

Choosing the right salespeople is essential when a company decides to open new territories. If it is an area previously covered by manufacturer's reps or distributors, the chosen individuals will at least have a base of customers to build on. If it is virgin territory, they will have to start from scratch.

Ideally the people chosen will be confident, experienced and convinced that the opportunity offered is sufficiently great to enable them achieve and surpass their earnings goals. It will be a big advantage if they are among those rare individuals who are constantly concerned with improving their lot in life. The sales manager will attempt to find individuals who are amenable to direction, receptive to help offered from the district office. They should have demonstrated ability in opening new accounts, missionary work and meeting the public in general. They are willing to locate in new parts of the country, and above all they will be no strangers to hard work.

If the company is fortunate enough to discover people with these attributes, it must treat them as they deserve to be treated. They should be guaranteed their average earnings during the previous year or two for a period sufficient for them to build earnings from the new territory to that figure. Further, they should be a continuing concern of their sales manager while they develop the business. As Willy Loman said, selling is a lonely job, especially if a rep is in a new environment, far from friends and close business connections.

An effective sales manager should do everything possible to ease the path of a salesperson opening a new territory. He or she will already have pinpointed the principal prospective customers, know their probable needs, and learned the names of purchasing department heads. The manager might have made appointments for a get-acquainted visit and will be sure to accompany the salesperson on the inaugural trip through the territory.

Coddling? Not at all: it is as important to the sales manager as it is to the salesperson to get the enterprise off to a good start. Making the trip provides an opportunity for the manager to establish rapport with and demonstrate an interest in and concern for the rep. Few individuals are so mentally strong they can sail into a new job in unfamiliar surroundings without appreciating the presence and encouragement of a friendly ally, particularly if that ally is the boss. Consideration is a quality much appreciated by everyone and personal relationships can be an important bond between the sales manager and the staff.

Territorial Realignment

Let us discuss redefinition of an existing territory. First of all, why should a territory be tampered with? Perhaps the area has enjoyed unusually rapid growth; many businesses including a number of potential customers have moved in. As a result the market for a particular company may have expanded substantially.

The salesperson in the territory may have grown too, but not at a pace equal to the region. On the other hand, he or she may have become complacent, content to skim the cream off the top and neglect other responsibilities such as missionary work and soliciting new accounts. But even the best salesperson, working as hard as possible, may not be able to provide adequate service to everyone in the territory. It may be the individual's best effort—but it is not good enough.

Should the territory have grown to the extent that it can support a second rep, one should be added and the territory divided between the two. Should an adjoining territory be subject to the same conditions and should neither be able to support a second rep, a third territory with acceptable potential could be created from sections of each existing territory.

In either situation attention should be given to the compensation plans of all employees involved in the switch. The resident salesperson who has lost a substantial number of accounts should be protected while he or she develops a smaller territory more effectively. It will take time to bring this rep's earnings up to average, perhaps six months or even a year. During a selected period, the rep could be guaranteed average earnings over the equal preceding period. The same arrangement could be made available to reps moved to the newly formed territories.

At the beginning of the changeover it would be important for the old salesperson to introduce the new one to the existing accounts. The fact that his or her earnings are protected during the changeover should make performing this important task easier. Of course, the sales manager would have the responsibility of seeing that both reps, old and new, get off to a good start.

It is one of the immutable facts of sales that reps will earn what they want to earn—provided, of course, that the sales potential is there. They will do this even though they really have to exert themselves in a relatively poor territory. Likewise, in the richest of territories many reps will work just hard enough to meet their earnings goal. Some earn $20,000 a year, others $30,000; still others $50,000. No matter where they are, their inclination is to earn that amount and little more. No one knows why this is so, but it is a fact. One of the toughest jobs a sales manager has is to develop a $30,000 rep into a $40,000 rep. Success in such an endeavor is one of the greatest rewards the manager can experience.

What we have said here goes for a surprisingly large number of salespeople, but fortunately not for all of them. There is a group of highly motivated reps whose constant goal is to do better for themselves and their families, who consider their present jobs not as an end, but merely as stepping stones in their path to the top. These are the individuals who lift themselves by their own bootstraps through increasing earnings into the upper echelon of management. More power to them: they deserve everything they achieve.

At times the potential of a territory outgrows the aspirations of a salesperson, but not to the extent that dividing the territory is justified. More satisfactory results might be obtained by switching assignments so that territorial potential is more in line with the earnings objectives of the sales staff.

Territories sometimes lose rather than gain in potential. Industrial customers close factories or reduce output. Changes in technology make some end products obsolete with the result that a territory, no matter how adequately covered, can no longer support a salesperson even of a low earning capacity. The only alternative a company has is to break up the territory and assign segments to adjacent ones. The displaced salesperson can be moved to a different area. Should the drop in potential be severe enough that continued coverage is not profitable under normal selling policy, the company might consider using manufacturer's reps or distributors to service existing accounts.

Matching Territories with Staff

This is a serious subject and should not be treated lightly, but before we go into a discussion of the matter let's indulge our fancy for a minute or two. We'll start by assuming that a corporation develops a group of products totally unlike its regular line and decides to market them in twelve territories. A like number of salespeople are transferred to the new division. The sales executive in charge of the project has the problem of assigning one salesperson to each of the territories.

The executive approaches the task with misgivings. Should Rep A be placed in territory 4 or assigned to territory 6, with 4 going instead to Rep B? How many possible combinations of reps and territories can there be?

Having earned an MBA from one of the major business schools, the executive recalls the principles of linear programming, the science of quantifying combinations and permutations. A few minutes of research on the computer reveals the awful truth: there are exactly 479,001,600 possible assignments in placing twelve reps in twelve territories. It's a fact. If you don't believe me, ask any mathematically minded friend to check the figure.

Our harried executive lacks the time to explore and analyze each option, but must make a decision, and soon.

Therefore he lists the characteristics of each territory as he perceives it and does the same for the dozen reps assigned to him. The more he knows of the reps and the area, the better will be his judgment in making assignments.

The following chart suggests a few of the points he will consider. The sales executive will add many more and go into as much detail as possible with the available information. Basically:

Territories Can Be	*Salespeople Can Be*
Good, poor, average	Good, poor, average
Of different shapes, sizes terrain or climate	Young, old, experienced, inexperienced
Principally urban or rural	Climbing the ladder or sliding down
Varied in sales potential	
Varied in number and size of possible accounts	Of different types; suited to city dwelling or country dwelling
Subject to special or unusual economic conditions	Of different personalities; leaders, followers, highly motivated, relatively unambitious plodders, fiercely independent or amenable to direction and control
Strongly or poorly covered by competition	
	Skimmers or diligent in performing all the prescribed functions of their jobs

---

When his lists are complete, the manager starts to fill square holes with square pegs, round holes with round pegs. Many assignments will be obviously right; a few might be open to question; but time constraints do not permit the executive to check even a handful of the multitude of alternatives. He makes his assignments and that is the end of the matter for the time being. If his preparation and analysis were thorough his decisions will prove wise ones.

Mismatches of Territories and Staff

It frequently becomes apparent that mismatches exist in a district. One rep might work diligently in a poor territory producing an unexpectedly high percentage of potential, but still not be able to earn the return his or her efforts justify. Another might earn much more, despite working at a more leisurely pace because of the richness of the territory. Here are a few instances where reassigning reps might be justified:

1. A rising star is trapped in a territory with low potential, his or her advancement blocked because of the lack of opportunity.

   Why not replace this rep with a new rep still on salary or drawing account? It might be an excellent location to learn the business. The present incumbent could be shifted to a territory more compatible with his or her talents.

2. A territory with good and still growing potential is covered by a plodder, content with present earnings, who cannot be motivated to develop further the sales opportunities available.

   Why not transfer this rep to a mature territory of limited growth potential? He or she can be expected to continue to do the job at least as well as before; that is all the territory needs. Sales will not drop, nor will the rep's earnings. At the same time a rep on the way up who deserves the opportunity could be placed in this territory instead.

3.　A territory might be small, compact, well developed, but of limited potential. It would make an excellent spot for an older, still effective rep close to retirement. Put this rep in the territory, and reassign the present incumbent.

In general, an analysis of personnel and territories may disclose that there are mismatches. Superior reps might have inferior territories. Switching reps would seem warranted if the company had the normal objective of increasing sales. Another consideration is also involved here. Superior salespeople will not long remain with a company that ignores their claim to opportunity commensurate with their ability. Companies cannot afford to lose their best reps to avoid upsetting less capable ones.

The best deserve the best. If the top producers don't receive the plums, disruption results and a salesforce can be torn asunder.

Rewarding the best seems a simple enough task, but actually it isn't as simple as it sounds. How do you define "best"? One individual is outstanding in getting sales, another can conjure up new accounts seemingly out of thin air, a third hasn't lost an account or received a customer complaint in years, a fourth has personally trained a half dozen reps who are now setting sales records in other parts of the country.

And territories: one is rich in profitable accounts, in another the sales potential will increase at a 15 percent rate over the next ten years. Still another is experiencing a slow but steady economic erosion that will soon have a devastating effect on sales.

All this reinforces the statement that many factors must be analyzed before a decision is made to reassign men to new territories.

Change for the Sake of Change

Some authorities recommend a policy of periodically switching personnel. They claim a new perspective, a new approach, can be beneficial. A rep too long on the same job loses zest, falls into a rut and becomes content to remain within its confines.

A new rep may be more amenable to direction if the switch is a step upward. He or she possibly will be more diligent in opening new accounts and doing missionary work. Complacent, satisfied reps will be shaken up, re-energized. People do become indifferent—new faces and approaches are necessary.

The opposing authorities are equally vehement. Stability and security are shaken by change, they state. Old relationships are broken. It is human nature to resist change and unreasoned change leads to unrest, loss of morale. Changing territories requires families to move, children to change schools—a traumatic experience for everyone involved in the process.

I feel it is important to examine this question carefully. I have seen people ruined as a result of being switched to a new territory and I have seen others who destroyed themselves on a job who might have been saved had they been

---

Change for the Sake of Change

Positive Results	*Negative Results*
Perspective and attitude change in new environment	Sense of security is shaken
A new challenge should stimulate complacement reps	Severing longstanding relationships destroys sense of belonging
New surroundings, new faces, get a rep out of a rut	Family life disrupted, roots are torn up
A transfer might cause a rep to reassess past performance and turn over a new leaf	Moves especially hard on children
	Morale often lowered
	The salesperson is confused— "What did I do wrong? Why am I being moved?"

---

moved. Let's start by listing the pros and cons of random switching.

Neither side is entirely right or wrong. Personally, I feel no change should be made based wholly on change for the sake of change. Changes should be made if a situation has deteriorated to a point that there is no hope of correcting it without a change and if there is a reasonable probability that the change will provide a successful solution to the problem.

Some changes will not be as unsettling as others. Moving a household from one location to another is expensive and harder for a family to handle emotionally than one that requires only that a rep going to work in the morning head east instead of west. Such a change will primarily affect the rep, but what upsets the rep may upset his or her whole family.

Only if a heavy preponderance of evidence favors the change should it be made. And remember, salespeople and their families are not draft animals, content as long as they receive their daily bread.

A sales manager having serious problems with Rep A and considering shifting territories might prepare a chart, such as below, to help determine what to do.

Problems	*Effect of Reassignment*
Sales less than satisfactory	Will start with a clean slate
Attitude not positive	Opportunity to leave behind
Relations with customers in some cases strained	negative attitude and get back to positive approach to job
Interest in job waning	Chance tp prove ability anew,
Lack of attention to new accounts, missionary work, servicing accounts	away from past failure
Complacency	Restored opportunity for advancement
Behavior might be influenced by poor choice of friends or unwise relationships formed	

Suppose that numerous talks with the man in the past year have not resulted in noticeable improvement in performance.

The sales manager is forced to conclude that if matters proceed in the present direction, the rep will have to be terminated. He has been with the company for almost ten years and during much of that time has done a better-than-average job. His past service and his tenure with the company entitle him to consideration. He is a person worth saving and should be given another chance in a new location. If he succeeds all is well; if he fails again he must go.

The sales manager decides to make the switch in territory, and calls the rep to explain the change and make him understand quite clearly that if his attitude and performance improve he is assured of holding his job. He must be aware that another failure will make it impossible for him to remain with the company.

I would approve such a transfer. It does not, of course, represent a switch for the sake of switching. There are many good reasons why the change should be made; I feel that equally good reasons should exist before *any* individual is moved to another location.

Changes are unsettling. Too many can damage a salesforce. Act only when action is necessary. Keep your sales staff abreast of company policy, let them know at all times how they are doing and what the future might have in store for them. Praise when praise is due, but when censure is required don't fail to deliver it. Finally, level with your staff. Total honesty is not the best policy, it is the *only* policy when dealing with people.

Companies rock along on the momentum supplied by the hard-working average sales staff, but expansion and growth come from the added impetus supplied by the top performers. I repeat, to get the best out of both territories and personnel, a sales manager must be able to fit round pegs in round holes, square pegs in square holes. The more a sales manager knows about territories to be opened or reshuffled and the more he or she knows of the personality and qualities of the salesforce, the better is the likelihood of making superior decisions on assignments.

Before going on to the next point let me make an observation. We have already talked about the experts who are preoccupied with the conviction that the best salesperson should always be encouraged to get promoted into higher prestige management jobs. Here again the word *best* intervenes—the "best" salesman might be one who has an order book at hand and a full tank of gas in the car who leaves in the morning and comes back with a sheaf of orders. Would that rep necessarily be the best at analyzing the competition, territory potential and attainable market share? Would he or she possess all the other characteristics a sales manager should have? It cannot be assured that it would prove so.

Using Commission Rates to Equalize Territories

Equalization of territories can be achieved by varying commission rates. Let us consider two territories (see illustration).

Territory 1

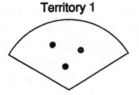

Highly industrialized
Small, compact
Three major cities
High potential - 9 on scale
of 10

Territory 2

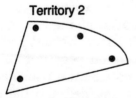

Mainly rural
Large, spread out
Four widely separated cities
Low potential - 6 on scale
of 10

The rep covering territory 1 can be home every night. No account is more than an hour's drive from home.

The rep in territory 2 is not so fortunate. Hundreds of miles of driving each week are required, widely scattered, potential is not good and expenses are high since the rep is away from home so many nights.

We all acknowledge that just as no two territories are similar, so also no two salespeople are similar. The rep in territory 1 might be a top quality old-timer who earned the right to a good territory by paying dues for years in territories like number 2. The rep in territory 2 might be a new recruit just starting to rise in the organization. No argument on this so far.

Some might take the attitude, "So what, who says it's got to be fair? That's how the cookie crumbles. Take it or leave it." Yet, equity may suggest some commission differential in territory 2. The salesperson might be required to pay expenses, and commission rates could be increased to compensate. Expenses would then become a variable cost rather than fixed. The commission increase might be great enough to cover the rep's expenses and leave something over as well. I am sure the company would not object, provided the rep did the expected entertaining. That isn't a problem when company money is used, but salespeople might develop a latent sense of conservatism when spending their own money.

The company has an obligation to pay the rep in territory 2 an adequate income, provided he or she does an acceptable job. What arrangement it makes is immaterial so long as the rep is provided an opportunity to earn a living.

Incidentally, surveys have indicated that older, more experienced commission-paid salespeople prefer to pay their own expenses and receive higher commission rates to compensate. Newer, less experienced reps prefer that the commission rate be lower, with the company being responsible for expenses.

Hints to Sales Managers

- Follow the seven steps when considering expansion into a new area.
- Optimism is great, but don't let your emotions color your judgment.
- When opening a new territory, research the individual you pick for the job as thoroughly as you analyze the area itself.
- When you cut a rep's territory, particularly one who has done a good job in the past, he or she deserves consideration. Be sure to provide it.
- Remember that while a sales manager's primary responsibility is to get sales for the company it is also of utmost importance to be the ally of the sales staff in helping them to do the best job they can do for themselves.
- Reassigning reps to different territories may be necessary, but never move hastily, without carefully checking all factors involved.

CHAPTER 11
Quotas

CHAPTER 11

Quotas can be set at all levels of a business. Quite often they start at the very top. The brass at the home office set the company objective for the year at sales of $100 million. It might as well be called a forecast as a quota. A share of the total will be allocated to each division or region, broken down further until it reaches branch level. Every branch sales manager distributes the allotted total among the sales staff.

One major problem associated with this method of assigning quotas down the line relates to the validity of the corporate sales objective. If the figure chosen is 20 percent above the previous year's performance and there have been few changes in the overall situation that could affect gross volume favorably in the coming year, every quota down to the amount assigned to a salesperson might be 20 percent above the ability to perform. On the other hand, an overall quota set too low will provide little incentive for the various operating levels to function at full efficiency. In either event the company as a whole and each individual in the chain will suffer.

Another method of developing quotas is to start at the other end, with the sales staff. Branch managers set quotas for their staff. Totals are sent up the line through the management chain until they are finally consolidated by the company's director of sales. How accurate the company objective will be if developed by this means will depend on the attitude and competence of the line managers who set the quotas.

Some companies work it both ways. Quotas filter down as others filter up. If totals roughly agree, all is well; if not, it's back to the drawing board for top and line management until mutually acceptable figures are negotiated.

Quotas may be based on gross margin or profits instead of sales volume. Goals are set for regions, divisions and branches, and it is a sales manager's responsibility to establish quotas for the staff that will enable them to meet the manager's goal. Sophisticated accounting systems are necessary if each branch is to become a profit center and sales managers must be able to convert profit back into gross sales or gross margin when allocating quotas to individual salespeople. That isn't an easy assignment.

So much for where quotas originate. For the moment we'll leave top management to its Olympian detachment and get in the trenches with branch sales managers. Why quotas? What purpose do they serve?

If quotas are not well designed, they can be the bane of a sales manager's existence, the albatross chained to the neck of the salesperson.

In ideal circumstances a quota is an accurate measuring device to judge the performance of an individual, a group of salespeople or an entire branch. Also, if properly prepared and used, it can be a powerful stimulant to every member of a salesforce. Perforce, a quota should be equitable, realistic and at least approximately attainable by conscientious and intelligent effort. It should encourage the individual or group for which it is set to achieve adequate or, preferably, superior performance.

Quotas also serve as an integral factor in determining an individual's earnings. Generally, sales above quota command a higher commission rate or entitle the salesperson to a bonus. Many plans even start the extra compensation at 85 or 90 percent of quota and the rate of extra compensation increases as plateaus above quota are reached.

Only with regressive commission plans do rates drop once quota has been achieved. Quotas should stimulate reps to do their jobs better, not punish them for superior performance.

If quotas are set too high, the stimulating effect is lost. Who can get charged up about an unobtainable goal? Organizations that impose unreasonable quotas on a salesforce and then pressure the staff to meet them achieve only negative reactions on the part of the staff, overselling and, consequently, damaged customer relations.

Quotas can point sales efforts in directions deemed important to the company. For example, if a company feels it is necessary to add new customers it will stimulate a salesperson in this area if a goal is set and a bonus paid to attain it.

A quota is a useful device by which a sales manager can measure the relative performance of his or her staff. Quotas will vary, but each individual's quota should reflect the manager's perception of what the rep is capable of accomplishing, given the rep's innate ability and the potential in the assigned territory. If all quotas are set equitably, the manager has a built-in method of establishing the relative performance of each member of his staff by comparing the percentages of quota reached.

One thing a quota will not do. It can indicate which individuals have done well and which have done poorly, but it cannot answer the question why each rep performed as he or she did. For the answer to that, the sales manager must rely on his or her knowledge of the personal strengths and weaknesses of the staff.

Are disadvantages connected with the use of a quota? Some people say there are. They claim that quotas are highly subjective in creation and are an inaccurate base for establishing goals. The result of a poor quota can be damage to a salesforce. They are right but only if the quota set is inaccurate. Good sales managers set accurate and realistic quotas.

Another complaint is that installing and operating a quota system puts workload on a sales manager. So what? Sales managers are paid to work.

The third complaint is that quotas impose high pressure on salespeople to the detriment of their performance. I don't buy this either. People cannot work efficiently and effectively if they are not aware of what is expected of them. If quotas have been set fairly and are realistically attainable, I see no reason for salespeople to feel over-pressured. Again, it is up to the sales manager to get the quotas right. If that manager can't, it's time to get someone on the job who can.

One last point before we talk about setting up a quota. Quotas will be effective aids in supplying incentive to the staff, especially when a substantial part of their compensation stems from commission. When a bonus is the prize for attainment of a quota it provides an even greater stimulant. I won't go into the argument about whether a sense of achievement or crass material reward is the most powerful motivator. Give a person opportunity to gain both and you can't lose.

To be effective, quotas must be understood and accepted by salespeople. Acceptance is of vital importance; people won't work for something they don't believe in. Wise managers will go over each individual's quota, making sure he or she understands it and realizes what attainment of it can mean on a personal level.

Four bases are commonly used in setting up a quota system at the branch level. A discussion of each follows.

Anticipated Sales Volume

The sales manager estimates the volume of sales expected, basing this estimate on an analysis of the market situation as it presently obtains. In doing so, the manager takes steps similar to those taken when evaluating the potential in a territory. Among the factors studied are:

1. The total market in the territory or district.
2. The competitive position of the company.
3. The presently projected share of market that can be obtained.
4. The quality of the coverage of the market. This, of course, depends on a subjective judgment of the ability of the reps covering the area.
5. Past performance in the area. Historical data should be adjusted to conform with changes to be made in personnel, territories or company policies. The effect

of new products to be introduced, price adjustments and even expected economic conditions should also be built into the estimate.

From this analysis sales forecasts are made for individuals and for the branch.

Gross Margin and Selling Expense

These elements are introduced in order to ensure that excessive emphasis will not be placed on gross sales dollars to the detriment of financial considerations. Under this approach, adjusted gross margin on sales instead of sales dollars themselves is used as a base for establishing a quota. A careful analysis of the gross margin of company products will be made and the quota will be further adjusted through the deduction of sales expense, which in this case does not include the sales staff's compensation. This is how the computation sets up:

Gross sales	$300,000
Cost of goods sold	210,000
Gross margin	90,000
Selling expenses	10,000
Adjusted gross margin	$ 80,000

Refer back to Chapter 4 for an explanation of the method of handling gross margin used as a base for paying commission. Remember not to include compensation in selling expenses.

In setting up a quota based on adjusted gross margin care should be exercised that the multiplier effect is not ignored. Which would you rather have, sales of $100,000 with a margin of $20,000, or $75,000 with a margin of $25,000? Perhaps the addition of $25,000 of overhead absorbing gross sales may be more important than $5,000 gross margin. The question isn't always a simple one to answer.

Sales managers have to think as well as act; a good portion of their earnings may stem from the profitability of their branches. So, if you use this type of quota be sure to do so correctly.

Normal Nonselling Activities

Another frequently used base for a quota system is a measure of activities other than direct selling of a salesperson. These may consist of:

1. Missionary responsibilities
2. Demonstrations
3. Soliciting new accounts, reactivating closed ones
4. Setting up displays and other promotional work
5. Service and customer calls for help or advice
6. Training new hires

None of these activities result in an immediate pay-off either to the company or to the salesperson. Yet, the effort must be expended if the territory is to achieve its full potential. Unfortunately, the performance of these functions must be rated on a largely subjective basis by the sales manager. The manager can, of course, study a salesperson's reports for a basic count of time spent and calls made, but must rely on judgment to estimate the future value of the salesperson's efforts in these peripheral activities.

It would be a most unusual situation indeed if these factors were of sufficient importance that the quota for a person was based entirely on them, but an appraisal of performance on these duties could be given a weight in determining the overall quota.

Combination Quotas

Using more than a single factor on which to base a quota will provide a solid foundation for goalsetting. The broader and the more accurately computed it is, the greater is the probability of setting realistic projections for the individual and the company to achieve. Formulation of such plans is complex— much more complicated than setting a gross sales goal—but the results can amply repay the additional effort required to set them up.

Some facets can be given a priority rating if the weighting scheme is based on the relative importance of each element. The chart constructed here will illustrate how a combination quota might be set up. This individual achieved 96.5 percent of quota.

	Weight	Quota	Performance	Percent of Quota	Times Weight
Sales	45	$400,000	$440,000	110%	4,950
Gross Margin	25	100,000	80,000	80%	2,000
New accounts	20	40	30	75%	1,500
Service, training, etc.	10	60	72	120%	1,200
	100				9,650

The example placed primary emphasis on sales volume (45 percent weight), followed by a target gross margin of 25 percent (25 percent weight). New accounts followed just behind (20 percent weight) and the balance of the quota is based on service, training and so forth. The company should meet its objectives in each area if quotas are met. Indeed, quotas may have been set so that 90 percent performance is the realistic goal for the sales staff and the company to reach.

Let us take a closer look at the performance of the rep whose record is reported. She is obviously a good salesperson, but like many of her caliber she has apparently been concentrating on selling high-volume, low-margin products. Note she sold 110 percent of sales volume quota, but achieved only 80 percent of gross margin quota. She excels in the service and training areas, possibly at the expense of soliciting new accounts.

The chart contains much information useful to a sales manager when discussing performance with a salesperson. Computing performance using a chart like the example is purely a mathematical exercise except in the final category, where the sales manager will have to rely on personal knowledge of the individual and an analysis of his or her reports.

Naturally, each company will have to choose the elements to be included in a combined quota system and apply weights that relate to the importance of each company objective.

Quotas

From Salesperson's Viewpoint

From Company's Viewpoint

Let reps know what is expected of them

Provide incentive for attainment

Provide bonuses for superior performance

If set too high, will discourage reps, pressure them

If set too low, will cheapen sense of attainment

Provide a tool to measure and compare performance of individuals

Can direct sales staff's attention to areas important to company

If poorly designed, can have damaging influence on morale and performance of staff

Are a useful factor in setting compensation plans for individuals

---

Hints to Sales Managers

- Quotas should set realistic goals for the sales staff, not impose an unbearable burden on them.
- Quotas should stimulate, not depress.
- To assign effective quotas, you must first know the capability of your people, the level of performance that can be expected of them.
- Go over quotas with each individual. Make sure he or she understands what is expected, and what can be earned if the goal is reached.
- Combination quotas are hard to develop and administer, but may improve performance markedly. Be aware of the benefits that can accrue from them.

CHAPTER 12
Policy Decisions

CHAPTER 12

Special situations are always arising with respect to compensation of salespeople when a company does a substantial volume of business. We'll discuss several types of transactions that require special handling, but before we do so, a few words about general company policy on the occasions when compensation is affected are required.

Equity is involved, of course—equity for the individual and the company. So is realism. Some things are possible, others aren't. To assure a good relationship between salespeople and employers each must trust and respect the other. Each must believe there is a good reason for whatever is done, a reason that makes sense. Salespeople have rights, as do companies. Judgments should never be hasty or ill-advised; they should be well thought through before they are announced.

When policies are established, the salesforce should receive a full explanation so the reason for the policy is understood as well as its application. There will be no acceptance on the part of the salesperson without understanding. When that fact is ignored, as it often is, unrest and complaints are generated with the result that both parties suffer.

When Is a Sale a Sale?

There are at least three answers to that question and from the point of view of some salespeople it makes a great deal of difference which is chosen. The three options are:

1. When the order is received.
2. When the order is shipped and billed.
3. When the payment is received.

We are interested only in what effect each choice will have on a salesperson. Company accounting practices are a different matter and we will not concern ourselves with them.

An individual paid a straight salary is not overly concerned at what point the company decides a sale has been made, but a commissioned rep and one who derives part of some compensation from a bonus have a substantial stake in the decision. Such a person would like to receive commission and credit for a sale when the order is received. The company might feel there's many a slip between cup and lip. It would prefer to pay commission at the time the order is shipped and invoiced. The interval between receipt of order and delivery could be weeks or even months.

Other companies are even more conservative, paying the salesperson only when payment has been received from the customer. In general, companies adopting this policy are concerned with the credit standing of their customers or the possibility of cancellation of the order. Companies selling to customers of impeccable financial standing should have no qualms about paying a salesperson when an order is shipped and billed, or perhaps even when the order is received.

It isn't only the commission that concerns the salespeople. If they are paid on a commission plus bonus plan, they might need the sales dollars to meet their quotas in a period. Any delay in crediting the sales to their accounts may result in lower earnings for them.

Except in those cases where a long time elapses between the receipt of an order and its delivery, the policy of considering a sale made when goods are shipped and invoiced appears to be a good one. Changes in quantities and prices will already have been made and commission expense will be offset against receipt of payment for the goods. When an appreciable time passes before goods are shipped, a partial payment of commission can be made on receipt of the order with the balance due at time of invoice.

Only in cases where there is a serious doubt whether payment will be made or there is a real possibility that the order may be cancelled before goods are delivered is there a valid reason for holding commission until the invoice is honored.

As has been said, it is largely immaterial to worry about when a sale becomes a sales if the salesforce is compensated entirely by salary. It does become important when commission and bonuses are involved. Companies should establish a firm, clear policy on the subject and make sure the salesforce understands the policy fully.

Installment Sales

How does a company pay a commission on a $1,000 sale when the customer pays $200 down and the balance over the next eighteen months? In some cases full commission is paid at once; in others only a percentage of it is considered earned when the sale is made and additional amounts are paid as installments are received. The amount of commission paid up front depends on the size of the down payment.

It is difficult to set up controls under this method of payment. Administrative costs are high. Expensive, yes, but customers have been known to renege on their obligations and even disappear with the merchandise. That costs the company even more, especially when full commission has been paid. In such an event a policy should be established to cover the repayment of a portion or all of the commission paid before default. Further adjustment can be made depending on whether or not the merchandise was recovered.

One further comment: in some industries, such as house-to-house selling of appliances, where customer failure to meet contractual obligations is an unfortunate fact of life, payment of commission as contract payments are received can serve two additional purposes. The sales staff will be more interested in assisting collection efforts if they have a stake in the money collected. Also, commission receivable on a number of still-open contracts that make payments on schedule can be a strong influence to keep reps on their jobs—should they quit, they would forfeit the balance of their commissions.

Bad Debts

What happens when a salesperson sells a carload of gravel to a road contractor who then spreads it over ten miles of country dirt roads, then becomes insolvent before making payment? In this example the problem is compounded since there is no possibility of recovering the material.

The first question to be asked is: Who approved credit? If the salesperson was authorized to approve the creditworthiness of his or her customers, the company would appear to have the right to say that since no money was received, no sale took place and no commission would be payable. (I should hope that if a second disaster of this type occurred, the sales manager would have a few words to say to the salesperson.)

On the other hand, suppose the salesperson submitted the order to the office, which according to company policy approved all credit, and the office approved the sale. The salesperson would seem to have at least some claim to commission. The rep did the job: if the office erred, let it pay for its mistake.

These are tricky. Whatever policy a company adopts to address them, it should be clearly stated and understood by the sales staff.

Returns

Goods are returned for many reasons, including:

1. Shoddy workmanship, failure to meet specifications.
2. Late delivery.
3. Overselling or misrepresentation by the sales staff.
4. Change in manufacturing requirements by the customer.

No hard and fast rules can be established to fix responsibility for every return. An investigation should be made, the reason for the return established as accurately as possible and the party at fault identified. If the company is at fault, the salesperson should not be penalized. If the rep made the mistake, he or she should reap no benefit from it. If neither the company nor the salesperson is to blame, a suitable settlement should be made with the salesperson.

Should an old and valued customer return goods for full credit because of a change in manufacturing process or product, the company could, as a matter of good customer relations, accept the return and allow the salesperson to retain all or part of this commission. Yet, some companies have a firm policy of paying commission only when delivery is made and payment received. Again, let the company express its policy clearly and make sure everyone understands it.

Long-Term Sales

On occasion a salesperson might be fortunate enough to secure an order covering the sale of goods extending for a period of months or even years. If the rep is salaried, no problems exist. If the order runs to a lot of money, the rep is reasonably assured of receiving a raise and that is the end of the matter. If the rep is paid on a commission base, with or without a bonus arrangement, the problem of the timing of paychecks becomes complicated.

Let us set up a transaction and see how we can handle it. We will assume a salesperson receives an order for a ton of a certain material to be delivered each month for a period of five years. The present price of the product is $6,000 per ton and the contract ties future prices to an agreed upon commodity index. There is a provision in the contract that it can be cancelled by the purchaser at the end of the third or fourth year, provided a penalty of the value of one ton of the product at the then-current price is paid to the company. Let us also assume the salesperson is paid a 3 percent commission and receives a bonus if an annual quota of sales dollars is met.

Incidentally, it took the salesperson nearly a year to secure the order.

The question is: When should commission be paid to the salesperson and in what annual periods should sales be credited against the quota? For the sake of simplicity we'll assume the price holds steady at $6,000 a ton. The transaction operates like this:

One ton per month at $6,000 per ton	$ 72,000	per year
Length of contract	× 5	years
Total value of contract	$360,000	
Commission	× 3	percent
Total commission payable	$ 10,800	

To pay the entire commission when the first ton is shipped and add the whole $360,000 to the salesperson's sales production at that time would be unreasonable. After all, the order might be cancelled at the end of three or four years by payment of a $6,000 penalty.

Yet, for three years the contract is firm. In that period sales would total $216,000 ($6,000 a month for thirty-six months). Commission at 3 percent would amount to $6,480. Suppose the salesperson is paid one-third of the commission when the first ton is shipped and the remaining two-thirds in monthly installments as the goods are shipped. This is how it would work out.

Sales of $6,000 a month for thirty-six months	$216,000
Commission at 3 percent	6,480
One-third paid when first shipment is made	2,160
Balance of commission	$ 4,320
Payments per month for thirty-six months	$ 120

If the contract were cancelled at the end of year 3, the salesperson would be paid $180 commission on the penalty payment received. If the contract remained in force, he or she would receive $180 a month for the fourth year, and again in the fifth year if the contract ran its full course.

Credit against the quota could be handled in the same fashion. That is, the salesperson would receive credit for one-third of the total three-year dollar volume ($72,000) at the time the first delivery was made and an additional $48,000 for each of the first three years. In the final two years of the contract he or she would receive credit for $72,000 sales a year.

That would appear an equitable method of handling the situation. The five-year annuity feature would appeal to the salesperson, as would the substantial initial payment. The company would find the plan attractive: substantial front money for the salesperson and further commission paid over the life of the contract. That feature might be an important incentive for the salesperson to continue in the employ of the company.

The company could not be faulted for being reluctant to pay full commission on contracted sales for three years at the time of the first delivery. After all, no contract is ironclad; companies do go out of business. Basically, it is prudent to relate commission payments and bonuses as closely as possible to actual delivery of goods.

I am not offering this solution to the problem of paying commission on long-term sales as a panacea. Each company will adopt a policy suited to its situation. The suggestion is offered for the purpose of spurring each company toward finding the solution that suits it and its sales staff best.

House Accounts

Rule I—Limit as rigidly as possible

Rule II—Clearly define what accounts will be included in the category

Many accounts can legitimately be classified as house accounts. For instance, the owner of an auto distributorship personally makes a deal with a local auto rental company for a number of cars to be delivered each year. Credit for such a sale correctly belongs to the agency.

On the other hand, suppose a salesperson has been selling a company regularly and receiving steady, medium-sized orders from it. One day the sales manager receives a call from the purchasing department for an order of substantial size. In my estimation, to designate such an order as belonging to the office is a serious mistake. It was the salesperson's account— he or she built a relationship with the company and provided needed service to it, and can rightfully claim the sale.

An argument could also be made that a salesperson would be entitled to commission who had consistently been calling on the company and had not, up to the present, been able to sell it. The order, even if called in to the office, should be the rep's.

In general, house accounts are large and are developed by the sales manager or the home office. They often require special handling, and price concessions because of volume are not unusual.

No salesperson who develops a customer, should be denied financial reward, even though the size and complexity of an order is beyond the rep's authority or ability to resolve. It might be necessary to involve the sales manager, a home-office executive and factory engineers in the deal, but the rep started it all and should claim the sale. After all, aren't sales managers, executives and engineers paid to do their jobs and lend assistance where needed? Circumstances should dictate whether or not the salesperson should receive full commission.

Time may become your ally when resolving some sticky situations. Let us say that a salesperson has developed a territory with one extremely lucrative account, the handling of which is so complex that management is frequently called on for assistance. The salesperson has made a handsome income from the account and when he or she retires the territory is assigned to another rep. It is a rich territory even without the one large account. Under the circumstances management might transfer the customer to house-account status. There can be little argument with the decision, provided an arrangement is made to reward the person who is assigned to service the account. The same action might be taken if territories are redefined and reps reassigned.

If a branch has a large number of house accounts, it would not be surprising to find a degree of unrest in the salesforce. An excessive number would indicate that the company should re-examine its policy on house accounts. When the only objective of classifying an account as a house account is to avoid paying commission, the company will deserve the consequences of its actions.

Split Commissions

I condone the splitting of commissions only when truly necessary. I can think of two circumstances under which splitting is justified.

A salesperson calls on the central buying office of a corporation in Toledo and secures a contract for a piece of equipment to be installed in a plant in Little Rock. The rep is entitled to be compensated for the effort, but so is the Little Rock salesperson who must install the machinery and train its operator.

In another case a salesperson makes a contact and secures the opportunity to bid on a job. The sales manager is called on to make the bid, and in turn enlists the aid of factory engineers in modifying standard equipment to meet special specifications. Factory technicians will install the machinery when delivered. The originating salesperson is the only one of the whole group paid on commission, and has certainly earned some share of the commission for originating the sale—how much depends on the value of his or her contribution.

Splitting commission may be the only answer when more than one rep and one territory are involved in a sale. When such circumstances are frequent, a company should establish a clear and well-understood policy to handle them.

Unsolicited Telephone and Mail Orders

Many companies encourage small accounts to order by these methods. Not infrequently, inquiries come from out-of-the-way places and often it is not economic for a salesperson to schedule regular calls on such customers.

I see no reason not to pay the territory salesperson full commission on these sales. Who knows—a follow-up call might result in additional sales. To call these found sales house accounts is a contemptible display of parsimony.

Commission Pools

Many sales managers throw extra commissions into a pool to be distributed among salespeople. These monies can come from several sources.

In some cases territories are not rigidly defined and several individuals work in an area. Should a customer not previously called on or sold call in an order, the commission would properly be thrown into the pool.

A sales manager who picks up a modest order on the golf course Saturday afternoon might contribute the commission to the pool before assigning the account to a salesperson. A split commission share might have been received from another office and the sales manager personally handled the installation and follow-up. That commission, too, might be added to the pool provided the sales manager was thinking more of the staff than his or her own interests. Additional commission comes from a surprising variety of sources.

Some enlightened sales managers consistently allocate a portion of the commission not actually paid on house accounts to the pool. This seems to me a smart practice. It is a relatively inexpensive way to provide money for a prize fund. If the fund stimulates salespeople to better performance the results can be most rewarding.

The pool should be distributed according to an established plan at regular intervals or when the pool reaches a predetermined amount. It can be:

1. Equally divided among the staff. I don't like this method of distribution; each rep should *earn* everything he or she receives.
2. Raffled off. I don't care for this either. Prizes should be used as incentives; reward the person or persons who respond best to a challenge.
3. Offered as a prize, or prizes if the pool is large enough, for winners of a contest. Base the contest on whatever you will: the number of new accounts opened in a specific period, sales of a new product the company is pushing, and so on.

A contest adds zest. Salespeople respond to a challenge. Even if the prize isn't all that valuable, it appeals to their competitive spirit.

Trade-Ins

Every company has its own policy on handling trade-ins. It also varies from industry to industry. Many companies pay commission based on sales less allowances. This is particularly common when the traded-in merchandise is of little worth and is sold for scrap value. In other cases, such as in the automobile business, the trade-in has a substantial worth. Some salespeople are given the responsibility of disposing of trade-ins they accept; in other cases a different salesforce is employed for the purpose. Some trade-ins are sold "as is"; others receive varying amounts of restoration before resale.

Trade-in policies don't just happen—they become established after long and sometimes expensive trial and error. My advice to a company is to adopt the same basic policy that prevails in the industry and not to fool around too much with innovations.

Windfalls

We have left a discussion of this topic for last, and for a very good reason. You may already have inferred from my earlier statements on "excessive" earnings of salespeople and regressive commission plans that I am not in favor of curtailing earnings of salespeople as a matter of policy.

In general, the same thinking colors my attitude toward windfalls. Let us look at three types of orders that can be considered windfalls.

In the first, an individual calling on a regular customer secures an unexpected, one-time, gigantic order, the commission on which in the normal course of events would amount to $50,000.

Sales management literature is encyclopedic on the subject of how such a transaction should be handled. The majority of experts agree that the individual should not reap the benefit of this unexpected bonanza. They are the same individuals who favor regressive commission plans as a tool to hold down salespeople's earnings. There are valid arguments in favor of regressive schedules under some circumstances and even of preventing certain types of huge windfall payments. I can, however, accept no argument that would deprive a salesperson of commission in this case.

Attempts are made to persuade us that since the salesperson expended little or no special effort or had little influence in securing the order, he or she is not entitled to the commission. If effort is the criterion for compensation, why doesn't a company reward a salesperson for the hours or days spent in a vain effort to sell a customer? The buyer was the salesperson's customer; the salesperson got the order fair and square.

There is no valid reason, ethical or otherwise, why the salesperson should not receive the commission. To make such a sale a house account and pay no commission simply transfers the windfall to the company, which did not create the sale.

The experts even object to payment on windfall sales because of the old argument that such payments might result in a salesperson being paid more than the boss. This, they say, would reduce the sales manager's authority and devalue the prospect of promotion to management. I have already addressed this fallacy and will not go into it again.

We are also told that paying one person a windfall commission is grossly unfair to others. How so? I'm not sure of the answer, but it seems to come down to the assumption that one person is not entitled to such a lucky break that is not available to everyone else as well.

I disagree; I should think the response of the rest of the salesforce would be, "Maybe *I'll* hit the jackpot next time." I *know* what the reaction of the others would be if the commission were denied: "Cheap chiselers"! Why should I break my back working for this company if when I get a lucky break they'll cheat me out of the commission?"

Another proponent of the restrictive policy fears that the sudden spurt in earnings might have a negative effect, resulting in greater and unplanned tax liability for reps. It might even cause the unfortunate individual foolishly to expect a continuing stream of windfalls and to start living above his or her means. Thus, for their own good it is better to keep reps earning at their regular pace and be sure you don't complicate their lives by paying them more than they are accustomed to. These suggestions merit no comment.

In some cases a so-called windfall may be accompanied by a request for a price concession. Terms and prices would be worked out by company executives and if a discount were allowed, the salesperson should be willing to bear a fair share of the concession through a reduced rate of commission. Notice, I said *fair*.

A final word on this type of windfall: for the mutual advantage of the company and the salesperson there must be mutual respect and trust. Destroy either element and irreparable damage will inevitably be done to both parties.

Our second example is substantially different. A salesperson calling on an established account is given a normal order and is then informed that a new policy of centralized buying has been adopted under which the customer will purchase all the requirements for five other factories in different areas of the country.

The salesperson should continue to be paid commission on all sales to the customer for consumption in the local plant, but there is no reason to compensate this rep for orders originating in far places and passing through the local factory merely for the convenience of the customer. The salespeople who covered those distant plants have a much more valid claim to the commission. They still call on the customer, service the account and, except for the change in policy, would continue to book the orders covering the plant's needs.

Should the other plants not have been customers, sales to them could rightly be considered house accounts. The reps asked to service these new locations should be compensated for their time. Undoubtedly they will rue the fact that they failed to make the plant a customer.

The third example is still different. The vice president for sales in New York meets the vice president for purchasing of a company with which little business has been done in the past. After golf at the National they hammer out a deal over a couple of drinks that will result in sales of above $1 million for a line of products never before sold to that company.

Such an account should properly be considered a house account and a home-office one at that. The district in which the merchandise is delivered has no valid claim to include the sale in its volume when bonuses for exceeding quota are computed. Again, the rep who services the account should be compensated for the efforts.

The cardinal rule on windfalls: be ethical, be equitable. Don't toss your money around indiscriminately, but always pay your people what they have earned.

One final personal note: many years ago the accountant of a firm that bought and sold paper in bulk to printers and publishers approached the president of the company and said that friends of his, a couple, were starting publication of a new type of magazine and wished to place an order for paper. Finances were tight for them, the accountant said, but he was positive the couple would honor their obligation for the paper. The owner trusted the judgment of his accountant and authorized delivery of the paper, adding that as the accountant had originated the sale he would be entitled to a commission.

The magazine flourished. Its circulation multiplied astronomically into the millions. Not too long afterward the accountant retired to a life of leisure. A windfall? Perhaps, but who was hurt when the commission was paid? A delightful story, and true too. Everyone was better off because it happened.

Hints to Sales Managers

- Be ready for problems before they arise. Do your thinking ahead of time.
- Know every detail of company policy that can affect your staff.
- Share your knowledge with your staff.
- "Why?" How often have you heard that despairing query? A decision is more likely to be accepted if the sales staff knows the rule on which it is based.
- Avoid surprises; bolts from the blue are viewed with cynicism.
- Remember you are the go-between—you represent both the company and your staff. You represent them both. Each has rights; make sure they secure them.

CHAPTER 13
Developing a Total Compensation Plan

CHAPTER 13

It's nearly time to construct a compensation plan from the elements we have been discussing. First, however, we should consider a few basic factors that will, to a large extent, control the design of the plan that will best fit your company. While we do this, don't lose sight of the three basic objectives of a compensation plan:

1. To pay an employee for service in such a way that reward is commensurate with contribution.
2. To provide incentive for salespeople to strive constantly to improve.
3. To design the plan so that it will be a positive force in helping the company to achieve its sales goals.

Keep these three objectives firmly in mind while we run through the factors that will influence your choice of a total compensation plan.

Financial Considerations

The company must survive while it is building a salesforce or entering a new market. If cash is a scarce commodity, the company will not be able to pay its salesforce a substantial salary and must rely mainly on commissioned representatives. On the other hand, when a new division of a billion-dollar corporation organizes a salesforce, its plan will be based on what is best rather than what is expedient. Few companies should experience difficulty deciding which category they fit into.

Nature of Market and Method of Distribution

There appear to be generally accepted practices in the compensation plans of a number of industries. For example, house-to-house salespeople for products such as vacuum cleaners, cosmetics and kitchenware are usually paid commission only. There are sound reasons for this.

At the other end of the spectrum are the highly educated, highly trained individuals selling expensive and complicated machinery or high-tech products. They generally receive a substantial salary as the major portion of their pay packages.

Whether people are expected to call on fifteen wholesalers or 150 retail establishments should also influence a compensation plan.

A company entering a new field should make a thorough study of the compensation plans of established companies already in the business. If the compensation plans of the competitors follow a similar pattern, it probably would not be wise for the newcomer to attempt to blaze a new trail. Experience will have influenced the others and one can profit as much from the experience of others as from one s own.

Nature of the Salesperson's Job

What is the relative importance of the various elements of the work expected of a salesperson? We have analyzed possible job responsibilities earlier in the book. Among them, some are better compensated by salary, others by commission. What is important here is to understand what the company is looking for and choose the most effective way to pay for it.

Compensation of New Hires

It probably would not be desirable to put inexperienced recruits just starting in a business on the same plan that is used for a veteran salesforce, especially if it relies heavily on commission compensation. A starter plan might be designed to carry a new hire through the training process until he or she could be expected to work independently in the organization. Such a plan might start with straight salary, and in a transition stage substitute a drawing account for salary until commission earnings could build to a suitable level.

Salesforce Profile

A company must be aware of the caliber of people it presently employs or intends to hire. Salespeople vary in age, sex and color, in temperament, education and background, in intellectual capacity. They have different aspirations. Some have an excellent idea how to fulfill them, others float with the current, seemingly unaware or even unconcerned where it is carrying them.

No company can construct a perfect profile of the ideal representative and hire only those who conform to the model. After all, blue-eyed people may have as many smarts as brown-eyed ones and, thirty years later, how important is the difference between a B and a $B-$ average in high school or college?

Nevertheless, there are differences between individuals of similar age or background. One may earn $20,000 to $30,000 a year while another makes three or four times as much. Don't make a mistake when defining difference by assuming the higher earner is the better individual. It may be so, but there is no assurance of it. There is a place for both types in our scheme of things. Any person, regardless of economic status, is a credit to himself and to society in general if he is applying himself to his work to the best of his ability.

What Level of Earnings Should Be Targeted?

Having completed our preliminary analysis, let's begin work.
The earnings-level target figure selected will be controlled to a
considerable extent by competitive influences. Certain industries historically pay more or less than others. Textile and
apparel salespeople are usually near the top of the scale; lum-
ber and building material salespeople much lower.

The government and many private research organizations
issue comprehensive statistical information on industry average compensation of salespeople. Even though the material
may already be a year or two old when published, it is highly
indicative of industry standards and trends.

Any compensation plan should be in line with those of
the competition. Markedly excessive pay for similar work,
while attracting the best quality representatives, would be
counterproductive if it resulted in uncompetitive prices or loss
of profits. Conversely, an appreciably lower scale would make
it difficult to hire qualified individuals and at the same time
result in the loss of experienced agents.

Designing a Plan

Let us look at an example of how a compensation plan might
be set up. First, a realistic profile for earnings of a prototype
salesperson will be established. We will pick $30,000 as a
starter; it may be too high or too low, but it will do as an
example. Furthermore, it is a good round figure that
simplifies the mathematics.

We will assume that the company in question has
decided to pay its salesforce a mixture of salary, commission
and bonus. Further analysis has resulted in the establishment
of values for the various functions the staff is expected to perform and has indicated the type of compensation to be paid
for each activity. That may sound complicated, but the chart
on the following page should clarify it.

We can see that the selling function is by far the most
heavily weighted (65 of 100 total points). We also note that

Job Requirements	Salary	Commission	Bonus	Total Weight
Training new hires	10		5	15
New accounts	5		5	10
Missionary work, promotion, servicing	10			10
Sales–adjusted gross margin	30	30	5	65
	55	30	15	100

more than half of the points (55) are allocated to salary, 30 to commission and the balance to bonus. Since the target earnings figure is $30,000, each point would represent $300 in compensation. Thus, a salesperson who performed every facet of the job would earn exactly $30,000, as follows:

Salary (55 × $300)	=	$16,500
Commission (30 × $300)	=	9,000
Bonus (15 × $300)	=	4,500
Total		$30,000

Observe—everything is in balance. How wonderful if only 10 percent of salespeople were!

Analysis of Plan

We'll start our discussion with the company's thinking at the time it developed the plan. A number of factors come to light.

The company considers as most important the selling activities of its sales staff. Of 100 points, 65 are allocated to this function—65 percent, if you prefer.

Training new hires is an important facet of the job—15 percent. Opening new accounts and general promotional work account for the balance of an individual's responsibility.

When we look at the three components of compensation—salary, commission and bonus—we observe that the company expects that salary will represent 55 percent of total compensation. This indicates first that the salesforce is expected to be composed of well-motivated, high-caliber individuals and also that the company is in a stable financial condition. Such a heavy concentration in the salary area will give the company a high degree of control over its agents.

Almost half the salary will be paid for training, opening new accounts and doing service and promotional work. The salesforce is expected to earn bonus points for working with new hires and adding new customers. The company is doing all it can to emphasize the importance of good performance in these areas.

You will notice that almost half of the compensation for selling is paid by salary, the remainder by commission and bonus. The high share of salary should give salespeople a sense of stability and security in earnings, while the commission segment is sufficiently large to motivate them.

It is also evident that the company is putting emphasis on the sale of products with higher gross margin rather than on gross volume of sales.

One curious fact comes to light as we study the chart. A salesperson meeting the sales quota will receive a bonus equivalent to 5 percent of projected earnings. He or she can earn bonuses of similar amounts by meeting the performance objectives set for training new hires and opening new accounts. Ordinarily we would expect to see exceptional achievement in sales production rewarded generously. It is possible, of course, that the 5 percent bonus would increase should the individual exceed the quota. To me that is a reasonable conjecture.

It is also quite possible that this particular company is in a period of planned growth and expansion. Thus, trained new salespeople and an increase in its customer base are essential. I get the feeling that this company knows what it is doing and why it is doing it.

Quotas under the Plan

At this point we have formulated a basic plan, chosen the methods of paying compensation for each of the sales functions and established a scale of values for rating their importance. Now it is time to set up a quota system for these responsibilities, a mark for salespeople to attain. Quotas will be established so that if the salespeople meet them they will have reached the earnings objective set for them and the company will have achieved its own goals.

It is by setting these quotas and explaining them to the staff that sales managers earn a good portion of their keep. In one territory the resident salesperson has no knack for or interest in training new hires. It would be useless to attempt to force him to do training—would turn new hires off rather than on. Thus, the sales manager would transfer the points allocated to this function to another area where the salesperson's performance could be expected to improve.

What I am saying is that the sales manager must be prepared to hand-tailor the plan to the capabilities and characteristics of the staff. The better the job the manager does, the higher are the prospects of drawing the best effort from each member of the salesforce.

Hand-tailored suits fit better than ready-made ones. The sales manager's job is to work with the demonstrated strengths of the staff, rely on the abilities they have displayed and at the same time attempt to develop new strengths in those who have evidenced a willingness to learn and grow.

Of course, the size of an organization has a great effect on the amount of "tailoring" a sales manager can do. With a force of a dozen or so individuals, the manager can design a plan to each. Should the staff consist of fifty or more salespeople, hand-tailoring would be almost out of the question. Yet, the sales manager need not despair; the staff can be divided into classes and different requirements set for each class. (More on this later.)

Training New Hires

We might presume that the company is attempting to expand and needs to add to its salesforce. As a consequence, experienced salespeople who have a knack for this type of work are expected to take a number of new recruits in the field with them for specified periods of time. The trainer is paid for this work and would also be entitled to a bonus for at least meeting training responsibilities.

New Accounts

A quota would be set for each salesperson, depending on what results the sales manager can reasonably expect from the territory. The manager will be influenced by territorial potential, by the experience and ability of the individuals concerned and by any other relevant factors. A bonus would be paid if the quota were met or exceeded.

Miscellaneous Promotional Work

The only way a sales manager can monitor activity and performance would be through personal observation and study of reports filed by the staff. Not an easy task, but remember, more than half a salesperson's compensation derives from salary. This fact gives the sales manager the authority and right to control the activities of the staff.

How well an individual discharges his or her responsibility in this area will be a matter of personal judgment of the sales manager. The better the manager knows the staff, the more accurate will be his or her assessment of the job done.

Sales

The quota will be developed in line with the principles covered in an earlier section of this book. It will be based on gross sales volume less cost of goods sold less selling expenses other than salesperson's compensation (adjusted gross margin).

When a quota has been established, the sales manager will check selling expenses including expected compensation of $30,000 against the gross volume of sales. If total selling expenses as a percentage of gross sales are within the company established guideline, all is well. If not, it is back to the drawing board for the sales manager. Either the salesperson isn't being asked for enough production, or is being overpaid by company standards.

Perhaps the salesperson is somewhat profligate with the expense account when entertaining customers. The sales manager checks this possibility and may have a few words with the offender. Never forget, even though people are paid for accomplishing a number of duties, the money to pay for them must be supplied by the proceeds of what they sell. The company has no other source of income.

Let us now add some numbers to our example. Assume a gross sales quota of $450,000. Average adjusted gross margin for the company is 28 percent. Adjusted gross margin on $450,000 is $126,000. The salesperson, who is expected to earn a $9,000 commission for selling the quota, would be paid at the rate of 7.1 percent of the adjusted gross margin of sales made. ($126,000 × 7.1 percent = $8,940—short by $60, but who's perfect?) If the quota of $126,000 is met, the rep would receive the full $9,000. If the quota isn't met, the rep is paid 7.1 percent of sales made.

A bonus of $1,500 (5 percent of compensation) would be paid if the salesperson achieved the sales quota. A portion of the bonus might be payable on a lesser achievement—say $500 for making 90 percent of quota, $1,000 for 95 percent.

Bonuses in all categories may be paid on a progressive basis, that is, increased for achievement in excess of quota. For example, a salesperson is paid a combined commission and bonus of 13.1 percent on adjusted gross margin in excess of quota.

Application of the Compensation Plan

Assume a salesperson has an adjusted gross margin quota of $126,000 which he or she exceeds by $21,000. The quota for opening new accounts is forty-eight, but this rep fails to meet it, securing only thirty-four new customers. The sales manager reaches the conclusion the rep has done a credible job of working with new hires and is entitled to the bonus for satisfactorily fulfilling this obligation.

The rep's earnings for the year would break down as illustrated in the table on the following page.

I'm sure an alert sales manager would point out that failure to secure an additional fourteen new accounts cost the salesperson $1,500—more than $100 an account.

The subjective judgment of the sales manager is called into play in only two areas: training new hires and missionary, promotional and servicing work. Only in the case of training duties is a bonus involved. The sales manager should possess enough evidence to make an informed judgment on the performance of any member of the staff. The manager knows how many new hires were assigned to the sales staff for training and how many days were spent with them. The manager should also be in a position to know how effective their training has been.

No bonus is offered in the area of missionary work. If the sales manager feels that salespeople have been neglecting their responsibilities in the area, he or she has all authority needed to instruct the sales staff on what is expected of them in the future. After all, salaries can be adjusted, and if people are paid to do certain jobs it is expected that those jobs *will* be done.

		Totals
Training New Hires		
Salary	$3,000	
Bonus	1,500	
		$4,500
Opening New Accounts		
Salary	1,500	
Bonus	–0–	
		1,500
Missionary Work, etc.		
Salary	3,000	3,000
Sales		
Salary	9,000	
Commission	9,000	
Bonus	1,500	
		19,500
		$28,00
Commission and bonus on $21,000 sales in excess of quota at 13.1 percent		2,751
Total Compensation		$31,251

Benefits to Be Derived from a Compensation Plan

Both the sales staff and the company should profit handsomely from a well-designed and -administered compensation plan similar to the one used in the example.

The salesperson in our example will enjoy the stability and security of a substantial salary and will have a full understanding of the companys' expectations. There will be a strong incentive for the salesperson to achieve and even exceed the quota. Since the adjusted gross margin on the rep's sales rose to $147,000, he or she will be paid a combined commission and bonus of 13.1 percent on the excess of $21,000. I am sure that next year this rep will not allow a shortage of a few new accounts to cost him or her a bonus of $1,500.

The company maintains full control over its staff. A sales manager need not be reluctant to advise or instruct a rep who receives more than half of his or her pay in the form of salary. The sales manager will be able continually to monitor the performance of a rep throughout the year and will even have the means to encourage the staff to make required reports; how can salespeople expect to earn a portion of their salaries for promotional work if they don't let the boss know what they have been doing in that direction?

A well-designed and -controlled plan will do much to aid a company in meeting its selling goals.

General Discussion of Plans

The plan can be used for any level of earnings target. At a $20,000 target, each point would be worth $200, and at $40,000 twice that. Naturally, a company would exert great care in picking the components of its plan. In certain circumstances, opening new accounts might be weighted more heavily. Should all territories be well-manned and little expansion planned, training new hires would be relatively unimportant.

In situations where sales are highly technical in nature, compensation would lean even more heavily on salary and less on commission. On the other hand, companies finding it essential to increase sales would provide salespeople greater incentive by relying more heavily on commission and a generous bonus. Other companies with a narrow line of products, all carrying basically the same gross margin, might base commission on gross sales volume instead of on gross margin or adjusted gross margin. Still other companies, striving even harder to increase sales, could adopt a progressive commission schedule as quotas are met or surpassed.

In short, every company has the means to tailor its compensation plan to its needs.

Not everyone is capable of earning $30,000 a year. The sales manager is responsible for evaluating the potential of the individuals in the salesforce. In our example we picked an individual who, in the estimation of the sales manager, should earn $30,000. Perhaps the next person on the list happens to be relatively new, not yet fully experienced, but definitely on the way up. In the past year this person earned $21,000 and the sales manager is convinced he or she could reach $24,000 to $25,000 in the current year. On that salesperson's chart, a point would be valued at $250. Naturally, the sales quota would be compatible with the earnings target.

Flexibility is the key in any compensation plan. It's the responsibility of the sales manager to make correct judgments about the salesforce.

Company Preferences in Compensation Plans

There are statistics galore relating to company and industry preferences for various compensation plans. The one thing they have in common is their age when published. However, attitudes toward compensation do not change overnight and a tardy statistical approach is better than no approach at all.

Roughly speaking, a quarter of companies pay straight salary. Another fourth pay a combination of salary and commission. Almost a third pay a combination of salary and individually earned bonus. The balance use various mixtures involving salary, commission, group bonus, drawing accounts and whatever else strikes their fancy.

Almost all the experts tell us in no uncertain terms that it is the responsibility of the sales manager to keep selling costs to as small a percentage of sales volume as possible. Curiously, they talk very little about the manager's responsibility in the area of selling. In my opinion the sales manager's major responsibility is to get as many sales as possible in the territory through legitimate and ethical methods. The manager is, of course, interested in holding down costs, but not to the point that reps are not paid in fair proportion to their performance. No one should want to pay two dollars for an item worth one dollar, but no intelligent person expects to get something for nothing.

Classification of Sales Personnel

Any effective compensation plan must offer a just reward for services rendered. Every plan must start with an evaluation of each person on the salesforce. Some companies classify employees in groups, say A, B, C and D. Criteria for inclusion in a group might be:

1. Age.
2. Experience.
3. Potential.
4. Past record of earnings.

New, inexperienced personnel would start as class D and move up as their performance improved. If they didn't improve after a reasonable period, changes would have to be made.

The middle groups would include, in addition to those moving up, those nearing retirement who might have been transferred to more compact, mature territories. A substantial portion of Bs and Cs would be individuals of limited potential who can be relied on to do adequate but unremarkable jobs. This segment might very well be the backbone of the entire organization—uninspired but loyal, hardworking people. Don't ever discount their contributions.

Members of group A are the tigers of every salesforce. They produce—how they do produce! They can be and often are difficult to handle and get along with. Controlling them turns sales managers' hair gray and begets ulcers. But what do sales managers expect in return for their pay?

Companies using the group system might set it up like this:

Group	Compensation Range
A	$25,000 to $50,000
B	$22,000 to $27,000
C	$18,000 to $24,000
D	$14,000 to $19,000

Salaries, sales quotas, bonuses and so forth would be set up to conform. Again, the key to success is the sales manager's ability to assess the abilities of the salesforce and arrive at a realistic estimate of its expected earnings.

Can a Salesperson Be Paid Too Much?

Of course a salaried salesperson can be paid too much—especially if he is related to the chairman of the board! I'm not talking about this type of person, nor about the person who profits from a once-in-a-lifetime windfall or bonanza. I *am* talking about those few marvelous producers in whose hands customers become gold mines. Should a ceiling be placed on such a person's earnings? Here again I differ from those pundits who advance the same old arguments that recommend denial of commission on windfalls and approve the theory of regressive commission rates to limit earnings. They recommend that a ceiling be placed on compensation, that bonuses of top producers be cut. They suggest that salaries be raised almost to selected earnings limits and commissions and bonuses be practically eliminated.

I approve none of these actions. When the same experts preach the theory that it is wrong to pay a salesperson more than the sales manager to avoid undermining the manager's authority, demoralizing the manager and preventing top salespeople from aspiring to promotion to management, I shrug my shoulders and say, "So what?"

It would appear that those "authorities" regard sales-people and management as adversaries. They seem to believe that it is the responsibility of the administration to pay not one cent more than it is forced to pay and that salespeople should be prevented from getting out of line and are not entitled to earn as much as their rightful superiors.

What can be the origin of such thinking? Isn't this still the land of opportunity where people can go as far as their wits and ability can take them? I haven't once heard or read one of these advocates of repression state that a ceiling should be placed on what a person could sell provided the factory had no production problems.

Heavens no!—let the reps sell as much as they can, just don't pay them.

And the adversary attitude bothers me. Isn't management on the same team as the sales staff? Doesn't each depend on the efforts of the other to succeed or even to survive? Finally, the imposition of a ceiling on a salesperson's earnings is total-ly foreign to the philosophy of selling.

When a sales manager has properly evaluated the poten-tial of a territory using tested methods and an especially tal-ented salesperson makes mincemeat of the quota, flooding the office with an unceasing spate of orders, why shouldn't the salesperson enjoy the fruits of his or her efforts? The salesper-son isn't profiting at anyone's expense; the branch and the company share in the success. The sales manager receives a bonus and a profit-sharing check and the company profits in-crease once budget costs are met and incremental revenue rolls in.

Who loses? No one. Other salespeople have a wonderful example to emulate. The success of one person can be a strong motivating influence on an entire office. Profits come from sales made, not refused. Pay the person who makes them. A policy of paying lower commission rates on less profitable products is quite another matter and in many circumstances has much to recommend it.

Over-Rich Territories

Several writers on the subject suggest that if a salesperson has extraordinary earnings, *ipso facto* his or her territory is too rich or too large and should be restructured. This could just possibly be the case. It is the responsibility of the sales manager to see that aberrations of this type are avoided.

On the other hand, if the resident salesperson is actually doing the work of two people why should a change be made? What is involved is a matter of coverage. If a person is cleaning up by skimming a rich area, changes are in order. If he or she is getting a greater-than-expected share of the market in that area, why upset the applecart? If the star performer is a flash-in-the-pan, his or her earnings will soon slide back to normal; but if the person really is special, earnings will soar accordingly whatever the territory.

A theory is held that a salesperson makes a territory, not the reverse. There is much evidence to support this attitude. When a $30,000-a-year rep in a "poor" territory moves to a richer one it often happens that within a short period of time that rep will again be earning at his or her historic rate. Conversely, a rep averaging $20,000 a year who is transferred to a "good" territory might show a short-term spurt in earnings, but will soon relapse to his or her normal earnings level. This phenomenon does not occur in every case, but it occurs often enough to support a suspicion that salespeople have an inclination to maintain their earning levels irrespective of where they are assigned.

It is the function of sales management to match the right individual to the right territory. Perhaps a sales manager's greatest pleasure and satisfaction comes in converting a $20,000-a-year rep into a $30,000 earner. Yes, there is some joy in a sales manager's life and the good ones rejoice when they are able to lead an employee (and the employee's family) into a better standard of living. That's success, and that's what it's all about.

Introduction of the Plan

This is probably the most sensitive element of the whole process of developing and installing a compensation plan. It is a human instinct to resist change, and resistance grows in direct proportion to the importance of what is changed. Compensation must stand very high on a salesperson's priority list.

All organizations, especially large ones, would be wise to pretest a district for a year before installing a new system throughout the company, provided it represents a major change from a previous system. A careful analysis should be made of the immediately past period and compensation figured under the new plan for each individual. If application of the new plan would have resulted in substantial variation from what was actually paid, the cause of the aberration should be determined and a judgment made whether the difference was justifiable.

If the application of the new plan would have resulted in generally lower compensation, a revision of elements would probably be in order. If payments would have been generally higher for approximately the same work done, it is equally reasonable to seek the cause and, if justified, make revisions.

Some differences between the old and the new plan would be expected. If compensation under both plans were the same, why make changes? The new plan would have been designed with three purposes in mind: to relate reward with contribution; to provide incentive to salespeople to achieve even more, and to enable the company to point the salesforce's efforts in directions more advantageous to the company. To put it another way, the new plan should make it possible for a salesperson to do better by focusing effort in areas more profitable to his or her employer.

For example, a company might weight a plan in a direction that would correct a weakness in its marketing strategy. The shift from gross volume to adjusted gross margin as a commission base should be a powerful incentive to a salesperson to sell the more profitable company products. The effect of such a shift in salesperson motivation should not be neglected when projecting earnings under the new system and comparing them with the results for the previous year under the old plan.

Let us spend another minute or two on this topic.

The salesperson who had in the past sold a large percentage of high-margin products would profit through the new system. Conversely, the salesperson who had concentrated on high-volume, low-margin items would do worse. One would be happy with the new arrangement, the other wouldn't.

Yet the individual who contributed the most to the success of the company would be more highly rewarded for the effort and the other person, for his or her own benefit as well as that of the company, would do well to strive to improve. The company might with justification say that one person had been underpaid, the other overpaid, and the change in the commission base made to correct the imbalance. To make an omelette one must crack a few eggs.

Motivation and incentive are the keys. Give a person a reason for achieving a personal best. The company will profit automatically if the salesperson meets the goals that have been set.

Presentation of the Plan

Let us assume our sales manager has thoroughly prepared and is ready to proceed with the installation of the new plan in the district selected by the company for the test. How does he or she go about it? Send a circular to each of the eight reps involved in the change, announcing that on January 1, three weeks from now, a new compensation plan will be introduced? Add a short paragraph to the effect that if every salesperson puts his or her shoulder to the wheel for the next year, they will find that the new plan is better for them than the old one? I am afraid that some unenlightened sales managers would do just that.

On the other hand, a top quality sales manager goes about the introduction of a new plan quite differently. Well in advance of the change-over date he or she has:

1. Analyzed all the facts and figures for the eight reps in the office, including earnings to date (say through November 30) figured on the old and new basis.
2. Prepared quotas for the next year for the entire force.
3. Projected earnings for each rep based on recommended areas of concentration. More effort and attention here, less there.
4. Prepared a presentation for the announcement. When the sales manager prepares, he or she should *really* prepare. The manager is aware that, at least at the beginning of the presentation, the audience will be unfriendly. Everyone will resist change. A few will control their reactions and keep a relatively open mind, and their attitude will at best be one of wary skepticism. They will hear the sales manager out before they make a judgment, but if the manager doesn't have a good story, they will join the others who are already convinced that any change the company makes is designed for the sole purpose of cutting their earnings.

   In making the presentation, the sales manager will not discuss particulars about any individual rep. He or she will explain the plan in general terms, showing how each element fits into the whole. Experience has taught the manager another important fact not to be ignored when talking to the staff as a group: that is to leave company interests out of the presentation as much as possible. Salespeople worry about them-

selves. Their attitude is that the company has any number of people looking after its interests while no one is really going to bat for them.

Our particular sales manager has good rapport with the staff, and has always treated them fairly. They respect the manager, which is why this particular district was chosen for the test. Also the staff won't take the manager entirely on trust. The manager must prove that the new plan, properly used, will benefit them.

5. Rehearsed the presentation to assure it will be clear, concise and convincing. The manager will record and play back successive efforts until he or she is satisfied the final product can be improved no further.

The sales manager calls the staff in and introduces the plan. At the end of the presentation the manager announces that within the week he or she will discuss how each person will be affected by it.

The order of these meetings is of considerable importance. The sales manager has been sensitive to the reaction of each person during the presentation. It is not difficult for the manager to read the expressions and attitudes he or she observes. The salesperson scheduled for the first meeting will be a loyal and successful employee whose attitude during the presentation indicated a proclivity to change, or at least no strong opposition to it. The last person on the schedule has a reputation for opposing anything that comes along.

If a good job has been done in setting up the schedule and the manager handles each employee with tact and demonstrates how the plan can be an advantage if the salesperson adjusts to it, public opinion will swing over to his or her side. Grapevines in sales organizations are well organized and fully knowledgeable. That is why the schedule was organized as it was.

The manager will, wherever possible, arrange for meetings to take place in the salesperson's territory, which will be more comfortable than in the district office.

Once the plan is introduced and in operation, the job is not finished. The manager must be alert to handle any snags that develop, and must remain sensitive to the continuing reactions of the staff. The manager must also be aware to what extent each person is or is not using the plan to his or her advantage. The sales manager has been around long enough to know that if the sales staff is content and prosperous the company can't help but do well. Its profits derive from the success of its staff. Make them successful and everyone wins.

And now, to wrap up what I have to say, a few suggestions.

Hints to Sales Managers

- Realize that your employees are real people, just like yourself, not inanimate pieces to be pushed around on a chess board.
- You speak of "your salesforce." If they are truly yours, *you* have a responsibility to ensure they always receive every consideration due them.
- Salespeople and the companies they represent are not adversaries; they both pursue the same goal—success—and to achieve it each must place full faith and confidence in the other.
- Match reward as closely as possible with contribution.
- Earn the respect of your staff. Show them the respect they richly deserve.

CHAPTER 14
A Sales Manager's Response to Problems

CHAPTER 14

There are signals that should alert a perceptive sales executive to the need for revision in the company's compensation plan. Telltale symptoms will also surface when territories require restructuring or when the traditional method of market coverage, whether it be through employee salespeople, manufacturer's reps or distributors, should be changed. We'll devote the final few pages of this book to a discussion of how a sales manager can spot trouble areas and the actions he or she can take once they have been pinpointed.

Faulty compensation plans can be held at least partially to blame when:

1. Morale is low in a salesforce. Employees start to grumble. Nothing quite suits them; they bicker with management and among themselves. Some individuals feel that they are underpaid while others are grossly overpaid.
2. Customer complaints increase. Service obligations are neglected and salespeople's attitudinal problems are brought to the attention of management.
3. Turnover in the salesforce increases. The warning flag really waves when long-time, steady producers begin to seek other employment.
4. It becomes increasingly difficult to hire qualified replacements.

5. Sales decrease, share of market declines.

6. Salespeople's earnings do not keep pace with industry averages.

7. The number of accounts closed exceeds the number of new ones opened.

8. The sales manager begins to realize he or she is losing rapport with the staff. An adversarial relationship develops.

The list of danger signals is by no means complete, but it does cover the basic indicators that portend imminent collapse of a salesforce. Perceptive sales managers do not wait until a half-dozen warning bells ring before going into action; their fine-tuned ears pick up the first rumblings of unrest in their organizations and they take immediate steps to correct the situation.

The first move would be the most distasteful to them; it would also be the most important. They would examine, honestly and objectively, their own actions and behavior to determine whether they contributed in any way to the malaise of their organizations. Have they been:

1. Fair and impartial in their dealings with their staff, or have they been guilty of favoritism?

2. Supportive, or have they left the force to struggle along on its own?

3. Selfish or short-sighted when handling house accounts, unsolicited orders?

4. Truly interested in and concerned with the well-being of their employees?

5. Fully on top of all aspects of their jobs?

Next they would question whether company policies were at fault.

1. Were policies reasonable and equitable to all salespeople, or slanted to the advantage of some and the disadvantage of others?

2. If a major portion of compensation was salary, were amounts paid compatible with industry standards and were timely adjustments made in adequate amounts?

3. Were commission rates competitive?

4. Did the company compensation plan accurately relate reward with contribution?

5. Were territories constituted and assignments made so an individual could achieve a level of earnings commensurate with his or her objectives?

6. Were territories allotted on a rational basis, or did company policy unfairly favor one class of salesperson over another?

7. Were salespeople's expenses fairly and adequately reimbursed?

8. Did company policies on windfalls, house accounts, returns, split commissions and so forth irritate the staff to a marked extent?

9. Was the salesforce kept in a state of constant confusion by an unending flow of seemingly unnecessary changes in company policies and standard operating procedures?

10. If earnings, and particularly bonuses, were based on achievement of quotas, were they impartially and accurately fixed?

11. Did the compensation plan provide a strong incentive for salespeople to do better for themselves?

12. Were earnings of salespeople in line with compensation paid by leading competitors?

The blunders of sales managers and weaknesses in companies' policies are the major causes of unrest in a salesforce, but one other possible source of trouble cannot be ignored. I refer to the negative influence of a small group of salespeople, perhaps even a single individual. As a rotten apple can corrupt a whole barrel, so also can one disaffected individual destroy the morale of an entire salesforce. If such people will not change their attitudes they should be dismissed.

When the sales manager has isolated the causes for discontent in the salesforce, corrections should be made wherever needed. If the company compensation plan is the major culprit it should be reviewed, revised or discarded in favor of a plan better suited to the needs of the salesforce and the company.

Should a single salesperson be dissatisfied with a territory, the matter is important but does not justify a wholesale overhaul of a district. Isolated situations should be handled when they arise, but if dissatisfaction with territorial assignments is rampant, the sales manager would act as in the previous example, first determining whether his or her actions had been responsible for the negative attitude of the staff and then analyzing the effect of company policies to discover whether they were to a degree culpable.

If territories and assignments had remained unchanged for a long period, the manager would probably find that substantial inequities would have developed and many of the complaints would be justified. Should such a situation arise, the sales manager should bear the major portion of the blame. It is the manager's job to remain alert to what is going on in that district. He or she cannot be excused for failure to detect and act on inequities as they arise, preferably long before they reach the problem stage.

As we have stated earlier, territories change as people do. The matching process must continue unceasingly. Territories require redefinition; the objectives of some salespeople rise as those of others fall. A major part of a sales manager's job is to monitor the performance of each individual and to keep a close eye on the changes in the potential of each territory under his or her control. A competent sales manager:

1. Constantly reviews and refines estimates of territorial potential.
2. Keeps a close check on the percentage of potential achieved in each territory.

3. Relates a salesperson's earnings to the share of potential attained in the territory.
4. Knows how salespeople's current earnings compare with previous averages. In cases of persistent or abrupt declines the manager will discover the reasons.
5. Is aware of a representative's performance with respect to his or her earnings target.
6. Knows what percent of quota each individual will probably attain and the reason for superior or inferior performance.

This analysis will enable the sales manager to evaluate the performance of each individual. He or she will know which are overachieving and which are not performing as well as they should, and will recognize the individuals who have proved they can handle a richer territory and identify those on whom a superior territory is wasted.

The manager will also be aware of those territories that should be restructured: some divided to accommodate a second rep, others broken up and segments added to adjoining territories.

He or she will recognize when the time is ripe to discontinue the use of manufacturer's reps or distributors in an area and cover it with company employees. Conversely, the manager will be ready to shift to another method of marketing when an area becomes so poor it is no longer economic to continue normal coverage.

Forewarned is forearmed. A sales manager must personally accept the blame if the salesforce becomes disgruntled and, because of that, fails to meet the goals set for it. The only factors he or she cannot be held responsible for are declining economic conditions and the inability of the company to produce an adequate supply of quality merchandise to sell; everything else falls into the manager's lap. He or she shouldn't even be allowed to place the blame for problems in the territory on short-sighted company policies, even if they are principally responsible for the deteriorating situation. If policies are at fault, it is the manager's obligation to demonstrate the fact and continue to crusade for correction until it is achieved.

Harsh words? Perhaps so. A tough job being a sales manager? No argument there, but look at it this way: selling is a noble profession and a sales executive is in a unique position where his or her efforts can have a major influence in several areas. Success in handling the job means that customer needs are adequately served; the company prospers; and all the employees in the organization or under the manager's leadership have ample opportunity to achieve whatever goals they set for themselves.

You will always have problems. Handle them, but keep your eyes fixed firmly on the rewards that accompany the successful performance of your duties.

INDEX

A

Accounts new, 178
Advancement, opportunity
for, 9, 39, 139
Apparel industry, salary
plan for, 16

B

Bad debts, policy decisions
on, 157–58
Benefits, fringe, 9, 15, 69–71,
75, 91
Bonuses, 62–66, 72, 147, 186
discretionary, 64, 99
fixed, 66, 93, 97–99
general discussion on, 68–
69
office, 68
point system for determining, 95, 184

C

Commission pools, policy
decisions on, 170–171

Commission rates, 37–48,
94–95; *see also* Split commissions, policy decisions
on and Straight commis-
sion
equalization of territories
by, 142–144
fixed, 20, 55
gross margin concept of,
43–45, 46, 153, 184
hints to sales managers on,
48
progressive plan of, 37, 46
regressive plan of, 38–39,
46, 150, 172
sales volume the basis of,
37, 44–45, 77–78
Company objectives, sales
techniques to meet, 3, 8,
77–78
Compensation plans, 3–11,
93–99
age of employee a factor
in, 8
analysis of, 183–185
application of, 188

ABOUT THE AUTHOR

W. G. Ryckman is a former regional sales manager and officer for the Electrolux division of Consolidated Foods. A lecturer at the University of Virginia, Charlottesville, on business communication, Mr. Ryckman is the author of twelve books, including *What Do You Mean By That?* and *How to Pass the Employment Interview (with Flying Colors)*.